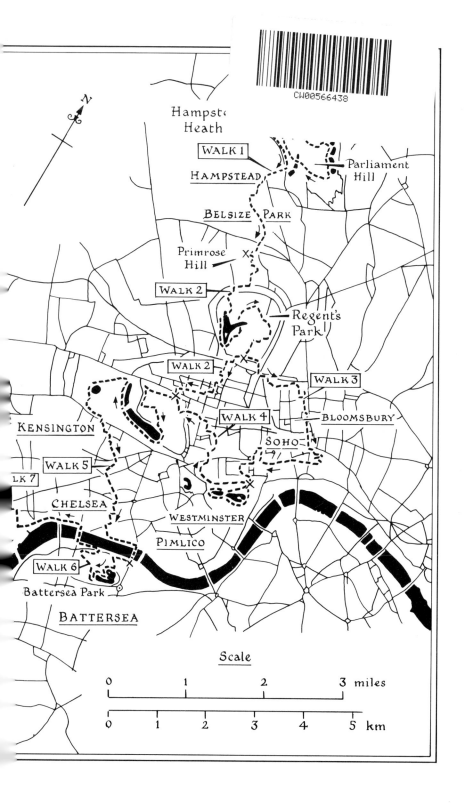

N

Hampste
Heath

WALK 1

HAMPSTEAD

Parliament
Hill

BELSIZE PARK

Primrose
Hill          X

WALK 2

Regent's
Park

WALK 2

WALK 3

KENSINGTON

WALK 4

BLOOMSBURY

SOHO

WALK 5

LK 7

CHELSEA

WESTMINSTER

WALK 6

PIMLICO

Battersea Park

BATTERSEA

Scale

0        1        2       3 miles

0    1    2    3    4    5 km

# Paws ACROSS London

*Also by Bruce Fogle*

GAMES PETS PLAY
PETS AND THEIR PEOPLE

# Paws Across London

## A guide for dog-walkers and others

## BRUCE FOGLE

Illustrations by
SUSAN HELLARD

MICHAEL JOSEPH
LONDON

MICHAEL JOSEPH LTD
Published by the Penguin Group
27 Wrights Lane, London W8 5TZ, England
Viking Penguin Inc., 40 West 23rd Street, New York, New York 10010, USA
Penguin Books Australia Ltd, Ringwood, Victoria, Australia
Penguin Books Canada Ltd, 2801 John Street, Markham, Ontario, Canada LR3 1BZ
Penguin Books (NZ) Ltd, 182–190 Wairau Road, Auckland 10, New Zealand

Penguin Books Ltd, Registered Offices: Harmondsworth, Middlesex, England

First published 1988

Copyright © Bruce Fogle, 1988

Maps by Peter McClure

Typeset in Great Britain by Goodfellow & Egan Ltd, Cambridge
Made and printed in Great Britain by Butler & Tanner Ltd, Frome, Somerset

A CIP catalogue record for this book is available from the British Library

0-7181-3204-1

Dedicated to my parents who by staying alive –
and together – for as long as they have – not the
easiest of feats – have allowed me to still think of
myself as a child

# Contents

# Introduction

## A dog walk across London?

In 1964, when I first came to London from Canada, I was appalled by what I considered the 'backwardness' of the city. No super highways or supermarkets, no shopping centres or 'downtown' parking lots, just old buses and taxis and dirty buildings. By 1970 when I arrived, as I then thought, to spend two years gaining veterinary experience at the Zoo and in private practice, not much had changed. I queued here. I queued there. True, some supermarkets were emerging, but not near where I lived. I had to shop locally, at the bakery, the greengrocers and the butchers. Something curious happened however, for, wholly unexpectedly, I found I rather enjoyed it!

The pace of life in London was different to what I had grown up to expect in Toronto, a very American, Canadian city. In Toronto you get your driver's licence at sixteen and then for ever more drive everywhere. Time is precious and not to be spent dawdling about on foot. London felt different. There wasn't the feeling of urgency here that I had always assumed was normal. Life was more relaxed. People walked more.

Much of this has regrettably now changed. Today, even native Londoners, not just the long-time transplants like myself, are prone to the contagion of urgency. Time has become money here, too. The Praetorian Guard of post-Thatcher Britain hop into their fuel-injected chariots at dawn and race off to power breakfasts. After a fast-food lunch they're back at their desks selling anything that isn't rooted into the ground as long as there's a good commission in it. The day is finished with a serious game of squash, and then a spate of hard partying. Even recreation is now earnest business in London.

This is the negative side of the Americanisation of London. The lifestyle has become hypertensive. The metropolis itself, however, remains as it was originally designed, for a more leisurely era, and is quite simply the greatest city in the world in which to walk your dog.

I don't say this in jest and I don't mean that London is the best city in the world for walking. Give me two working feet and I'll always opt for using them non-stop in Venice. But Venice is useless for dog-walking. There's no green space and, besides, dogs have to wear muzzles there. New York is rotten for dog-walking, too. New York has magnificent Central Park, but that's all, and it's only safe in daylight. Paris isn't up to scratch, either. Paris has marvellous open green spaces but there even the humans aren't allowed on the grass!

London is unique. Across the width and depth of London there are over sixty-seven square miles of public open land where you can walk your dog. That's an amazing amount of land, especially when you consider that the City of London, the financial heart of the metropolis, is only one historic square mile in size. There are over 1,700 public parks in London, each at least an acre in size, where you can walk your dog. Calculated in a different way, for every eight acres of buildings and roads in London there is an acre of public park. And on top of that, there is the myriad of private squares in central London for the use of local residents. When I lived near Marble Arch, my family, including my dogs, exercised in the three acres of Portman Square. We have since moved to Notting Hill Gate and now have access to Ladbroke Square, a verdant eight-acre private residential garden. One way and another, London is one of the greenest of the world's giant cities.

But why, you might ask, should I differentiate between going walking and going dog-walking? Both, it would appear, perform the same function. Walking gives cause to ruminate, to observe, to cogitate and to wonder at what you see: light reflecting un-expectedly off a building you see every day but have never noticed; a jungle of weeds growing on an untended balcony; butterflies clouding a stalk of buddleia; an owl hooting in a tree.

Dog-walking is the same but different. Several years ago, a social scientist came to my veterinary practice in central London and asked if he could borrow some of my clients. He asked them to walk casually through Hyde Park and, as they did so, he noted down how often fellow walkers either spoke to his subjects or acknowledged them by nodding or smiling.

Once this had been done, he asked the same people to walk the same route but this time accompanied by their dogs. Now, any dog-walker will know what the results of his observations were. When walking your dog you are far more likely to stop and talk to others, and others are far more likely to stop and talk to you. That's the difference between walking and *dog*-walking! Which is why I chose to walk with my dogs across London.

*Paws Across London* is the description of a walk along the most unexpected public footpath in Britain, a nature walk from Kenwood House at the top of Hampstead Heath to Ham House at the far end of Richmond Park. For my dogs, it was a marvellous way to meet others of their kind in distant Edens they would never have visited. For me, it was an opportunity to relax, to watch, listen to and observe both London and Londoners from a unique, green vantage.

I went on this walk with my two golden retrievers, Liberty and Lexington, and with my wife, Julia Foster. The walk itself was divided into seven sections. In addition, we took a two-section detour, a 'dog leg' if you will, through the squares and green spaces of Bloomsbury and Soho, and an extra walk, near the end of the sixty or so miles, around Wimbledon Common.

If you plan to take this walk through London yourself, make sure that you're in the right physical condition to do so. If you plan to take this walk with your dog, make sure that he or she too is physically prepared for the endeavour. Fit and active dogs will love the exercise. Slothful pets will hate you for forcing them to breathe fresh air. Dogs that are not in peak condition – the elderly and the overweight in particular – can be damaged by this type of exercise. If your pet is out of condition and you want to get him back to peak form, reintroduce daily exercise gradually – say fifteen minutes a day for the first few days, increased perhaps twice weekly till he is prepared for three to four hours of activity. If you break your dog in this way, you'll help yourself, too.

Incidentally, when I first mentioned to Julia that I was considering going on a long walk with my dogs, my first choice was backpacking for a week in the High Sierras of Southern California. Dreams are great. *This* is the compromise.

# 𝒲alk One

## Ken Wood to Primrose Hill

START: North Wood bus stop on Hampstead Lane, N6.

END: Entrance to Primrose Hill on Primrose Hill Road, NW3.

LENGTH: Approximately 6 miles.

TIME: Approximately 3 hours.

LEADS: Required in the grounds of Kenwood House and in the garden of The Freemasons Arms.

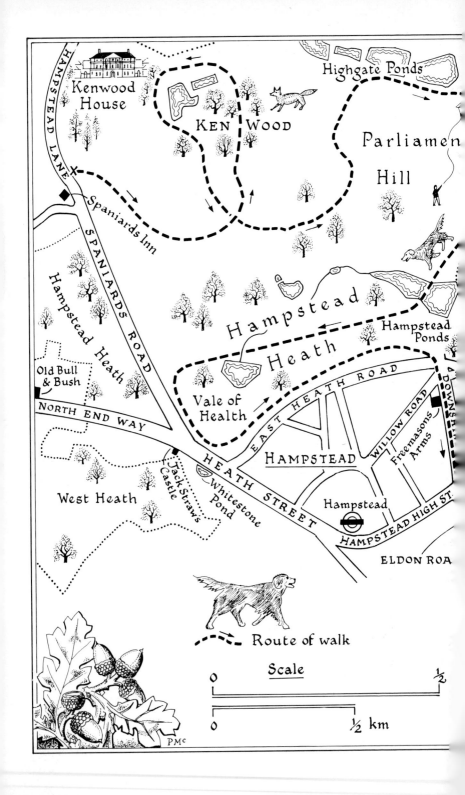

Kenwood House

Hampstead Lane

KEN WOOD

Highgate Ponds

Parliament Hill

Spaniards Inn

Spaniards Road

Hampstead Heath

Hampstead Ponds

Old Bull & Bush

Hampstead Heath

Vale of Health

NORTH END WAY

Heath

EAST HEATH ROAD

DOWNS...

Willow Road

Freemasons Arms

West Heath

Jack Straws Castle

Whitestone Pond

HEATH STREET

HAMPSTEAD

Hampstead

HAMPSTEAD HIGH ST.

ELDON ROA...

Route of walk

Scale

0                    ½

0                    ½ km

PMᶜ

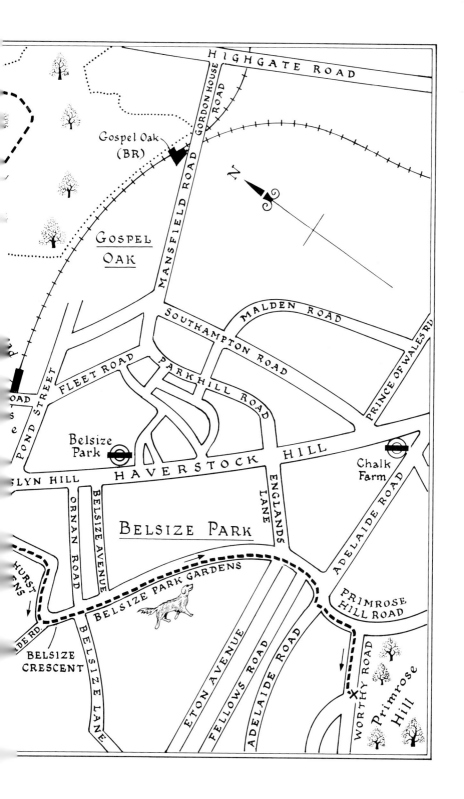

**From Kenwood House, through Ken Wood and Hampstead Heath, then Hampstead and Belsize Villages to Primrose Hill**

'We should have been here at seven!' my wife commented as I parked the car at **Kenwood House** and let her and the dogs out for a quick scamper about. It was the beginning of a casual and relaxing open-ended walk across London with Julia and our dogs and we were 'LATE!'

I put leads on the dogs and walked them from the **North Wood** parking area, down the right-hand path towards the wet western corner of Ken Wood called **Kenwood Farm**. Julia was free to scurry about filling her pockets with the early autumn windfall of acorns and beechnuts. Who exactly was I taking for a walk?

Once we were through the cattle gate, the dogs were allowed off their leads and they sailed gazelle-like through the air at the pleasure of free-range running. I walked along through the open field surrounded by red oak, birch and hornbeam, past the pine-clad hill separating us from The Spaniards Inn beyond and marvelled that I was in the heart of metropolitan London. It smelled like a crisp damp autumn day in the country. There had been a heavy rain the night before and the grass was glistening. Squirrels were everywhere, but Liberty and Lexington were too preoccupied with their own enjoyment to notice them. They had found a bog and were partaking in one of their favourite activities, wallowing.

Liberty and Lexington are both female golden retrievers, but the similarity ends there. At three years of age, Liberty is a bit of a benign tearaway. Lithe and muscular, she shares many attributes with my eldest daughter. Libby acts first and thinks later. She's naturally inquisitive, gregarious and a born athlete. Libby is the life of any canine party. Lexington, on the other hand, at one, is a born gentlewoman. She is a follower – awestruck by Liberty's outgoing and sociable nature but unable to build up Liberty's enthusiasm for activity. Whereas Libby will run until she drops and then keep on running, Lex will quite sensibly stop on occasion and become a keen observer rather than an active participant.

My dogs weren't the only runners, however. Only serious joggers and dog-walkers were in Ken Wood this early on a Sunday morning, except for one couple – but they were in love. Joggers, all plugged into their personal stereos, pulsated past us. Many were jogging dog-walkers. I was, of course, a walking dog-jogger, a far more sensible activity. Let the dogs act like idiots.

Julia marvelled at it all. Somehow, some way, we had never visited this part of the park. It was glorious. At the sight of our dogs, rabbits practised their 100-yard dashes into the distance while the dogs carried on sniffing trees and runners. A jogger sweated past pumping weights and exercising his white standard poodle. Liberty likes big dogs and started to follow, but was called back by Julia. I worried about the blood-red complexion of the jogger's face but was relieved to see that at least there would be help about if he needed it. Signs on the path marked out the route of the British Heart Foundation fun run. No doubt there were cardiac resuscitation teams lurking in the underbrush.

Liberty eyed a troika of wire-haired standard dachshunds, raced up and stood over them.

'Liberty! Come here!' demanded the pack leader and Lib returned to Julia's side as she apologised to the dachshunds' owner, an elderly dignified man with a cane.

'A bitch and her sons. I used to have smooth-haired dachs but these have less back problems.'

How right he was, but I wasn't going to get into the trap of letting on that I was a vet.

We continued along past the gorse and nettle to the iron gate to the left leading back into the wooded section of Ken Wood. Two ladies with two Labradors and a collie passed us. The Labs were carrying branches in their mouths. The collie had a lolly stick. I nodded a hello. What I wanted to do was show Julia what is perhaps the most glorious view in London. We walked along the path towards a massive beech tree, a giant of almost mathematical neatness whose flat roots reach out for yards across the sandy soil. Standing beneath the tree on a height of land, you see the most quintessential English view. If anyone asks why I still live in London and have not returned to North America, this is what I would show them. Look across a lush meadow, over a gentle valley, past a dense wood of red and scarlet oak and there, sitting on the rise of its manicured garden, is Kenwood House. Robert Adams designed the house in 1764, a model of Georgian restraint. Humphry Repton landscaped it, using to advantage the fragment of the ancient Forest of Middlesex in which I was standing and my dogs were cavorting. It is a lyrical view, guaranteed to reduce the blood pressure of the most harried Type A individuals and Julia

5

and I stood there enchanted by the sight while a Gordon setter wandered up to us and slobbered on my trousers.

The setter was shortly joined by its three Irish setter companions, all good slobberers but not in the same class as the Gordon. All four dogs now focused on my nether regions. I know that dogs have twenty times the number of scent receptors in their noses that we do and that almost two-thirds of a dog's brain is devoted to smell, but were they trying to tell me something?

'Liberty! Don't get silly!' Julia demanded as Lib sailed into the middle of the gathering. The setters' owner appeared, swinging the obligatory four chain leads. 'I'm so sorry,' he said and his dogs careened off towards the bog.

While Liberty explained to Lexington the nutritional value of rabbit droppings, Julia and I started walking towards Kenwood House, meeting two Metropolitan Police constables in the field.

They looked as if they were on a pleasurable stroll, not walking their beat, and I asked them if they had any serious problems to deal with.

'The odd flasher, a little glue-sniffing, but that's all,' was the reply of the taller one.

We continued walking with them and, fresh from the invigorating view from beneath the beech tree, I launched into an accolade of how magnificent Ken Wood was.

'Yes, and aren't the Saturday concerts in the bowl magnificent,' said the shorter constable.

I vaguely knew about the concerts but hadn't realised what they were.

'Glyndebourne's a lottery,' he went on. 'It's sold out months in advance. You apply for tickets in January and have a twenty per cent chance of getting any. But here you can come in the evening for a quiet picnic and then sit back and listen to glorious music in a magical setting.' He pulled from his pocket a map of Ken Wood and the Heath, as published by the London Residuary Body, and a programme for the Saturday night open-air concerts and handed them to me. 'I'll tell you what to do,' he said. 'A few rows of seats beside the lake are reserved and you can come into the bowl early for those. Buy one of them, take your picnic blanket and spread it out in the best spot. Your friends can join you later when the gates are open to the public.' I thanked them and we parted paths.

I stared squirrel-eyed at Julia. Had I heard correctly? Had a London bobby just told me about the tribulations of getting into Glyndebourne? Do I need to change my whole perspective of 'the law'?

Shouting to the dogs to get out of the stream where they were fishing for frogs, we reached the bottom of the valley and the edge of the lawn of **Kenwood House**. Dogs are to be kept on leads in the grounds of the house but along the bottom of the lawn and beside the pond I counted thirteen trotting around on their own. Lib and Lex were left to free-range it.

Julia and I walked along the edge of the lawn, beside the pond. The dogs made a dash for the water, washing off the last remains of the bog mud, then rolled on the grass. By now they had become accustomed to the numbers of other dogs and were becoming more casual and blasé in their meetings: a quick nose up the backside, then on with the walk.

We continued through the concert bowl, a sloping lawn leading down to a small lake on the other side of which is the orchestra site itself. I have always thought of Tanglewood, the summer home of the Boston Symphony Orchestra in Lenox, Massachusetts, as the ideal setting for outdoor evening concerts. And without the mosquitoes, built along the lines of Harrier jump jets, it would be, but the concert bowl at Kenwood House is unique in its lushness and its proximity to such a magnificent building.

I followed the wet footprints leading from the lake into the woods. Julia and the dogs accompanied. Julia resumed filling her pockets with acorns. I'm married to a chipmunk. She doesn't know why she's collecting acorns but, as certain as night follows day, she'll find some use for them some day! An anxious-looking wet German shepherd tore past us towards the pond and then back into the woods with a ball in his mouth. A very fat lady jogger jiggled past, the first person I had seen without a dog since we had entered the grounds of the house.

**Ken Wood** is a piece of dark deep oak and beech woodland, once in danger of being torn down to make way for urban development. There has probably been continuous tree cover in these woods since prehistoric times, a remnant of the ancient forests that covered England before farmers and dog-walkers arrived on this island. As I continued along, I saw that the anxious German shepherd had found his owner and the owner was one of my clients. 'Hello,' I said, and as I did so the dog spat the ball out of his mouth and cowered behind his master's legs. 'Recognises me, I see.'

'Hello, BALL!' came the reply, and the shepherd retrieved his fluorescent orange tennis ball while giving me a wide circle. There was no way I could explain I wasn't, on this occasion, particularly interested in his anal glands.

As three men with four wet spaniels walked by, we chatted about the glorious day but were interrupted by Julia's shouts. 'Liberty! Get over here!'

With my dogs, we only ever have to call Libby, the acknowledged leader, and Lex comes too. They had been rolling and Julia wanted to know in what. She bent down and sniffed Lib's neck, then reeled back as if she had been sprayed with ammonia. Liberty stood there wagging and smiling while Lexington sat beside her looking apologetic. There was no smell on Lexington. It was only Lib who had discovered such a delectable Highgate treat – fox droppings, the ultimate canine cologne! Now we were stuck with it for the rest of the morning.

I picked some leaves and rubbed what I could off her neck and continued on. Julia had temporarily lost some of the joy of beechnut-hunting but it soon returned. We emerged from the woods and found ourselves on the Heath once more, only a few yards further south than the beech tree where we had turned off a half hour before.

This is the part of the Heath favoured by the Hampstead intelligentsia of the sixties and seventies, ageing radicals walking ageing radical dogs and populating the Hampstead that E. M. Forster described in *A Passage to India* as 'an artistic and thoughtful little suburb of London'.

A Japanese lady passed, walking her cairn terrier. As she did so, the chief cried out, 'Liberty!' and our delinquent emerged from the underbrush where she had spotted a well-camouflaged short-haired pointer privately carrying out his daily ablutions. 'I'm so sorry,' said Julia, a rejoinder that was now beginning to sound like a broken record.

Continuing south, we walked across an open meadow towards a path leading south-east to the **Highgate Ponds**. The grass was deep and Libby stopped frequently to roll. Lexington quizzically followed, the young idolator copying every move of her knowledgeable elder. Wherever Lib rolled, Lex rolled. Wherever Lib sniffed, Lex sniffed.

The weather continued to improve, cumulus clouds and 747s scudding through the sky, when I heard bagpipes. As I reached the path I could see, on the crest of the hill, a man with his dog. It was the man who was playing the bagpipes. The sound was magnificent and I walked up the hill to ask him what he was playing. 'Dunno', was his reply and I backtracked and rejoined Julia and the dogs, all of whom were playing leapfrog over the ditch (known locally as break-leg gulch) that runs along the hill side of the path.

The grass had just been cut on the hill and it looked and smelled like new-mown hay. Both dogs rolled, but each time found themselves in the ditch. They ran back and forth while a lady smoking a Marlboro sat on a nearby bench saying, 'Hello sweetheart' to her uninterested Bedlington terrier.

It struck me that Julia and I had been walking for over an hour and a half and hadn't met any really interesting individuals yet. I saw a great-crested grebe hidden in the birch and willow of the first pond of the bird sanctuary at Highgate Ponds, but even that wasn't really interesting as they are now a relatively common sight there. They have become common because natural cover is allowed to grow and, equally important, dogs can't get through the perimeter fence to harass them!

It was 10.30 a.m. and the Heath was beginning to fill with people. Until now the number of dogs had surpassed the number of humans, but now more humans without dogs were appearing and the first pram had arrived.

Lexington did a bellyflop into the second pond and dog-paddled away in a southerly direction while Libby stood up to her chest, as always, struggling in her mind as to what to do. She wants to swim but can't, the only golden retriever in creation with such a disability. Liberty can duck dive and retrieve objects from the bottom of a pond, but only if her feet are firmly planted in the mud. Lexington started out as a young pup doing a simple dog-paddle, rapidly progressed to the point where she could tread water while waiting for a stick to be thrown, and is now perfecting her overarm backstroke. Liberty hates this perfection and lords it over the youngster when she emerges from the water, but this is one area where Lexington acts on her own. With the Nat West Tower glistening on the horizon, Lexington, two West Highland terriers, a German shepherd and a Hungarian Viszla competed in the dog-paddle in the men's bathing pool. There were more dogs than men in the pond. It always amazes me how such a disparate group as this – five dogs that have never set eyes on each other before – can convivially, or at least without aggravation, go for a swim together, each vying for the twig that an ever so obedient owner throws into the water.

The pond water washed the last traces of the Ken Wood fox off Liberty's coat and we continued walking south past the last Highgate pond and towards **Parliament Hill**.

Druids, probably accompanied by their Druid dogs, meet on Parliament Hill each midsummer solstice, but today the hill was devoted, as it usually is, to kite-flyers. Libby ran off to investigate a mole hill on the tumulus below the hill and started digging. Lexington decided this was an exciting venture and followed suit. Little did they know that prehistoric tribes, the first settlers of Britain, lived on this site. The legend developed that Queen Boudicca was buried in this barrow and in 1894 the barrow was excavated in a search for her remains. My dogs were now continuing that fruitless dig.

Julia and I continued up the hill westwards. The sudden skyline of high-rise flats and terraced houses comes as a surprise, but a gentle surprise, after the solitude of Ken Wood. Looking south-wards, it's a friendly city panorama: train tracks, a playing field and a sports track where the tin changing-hut that John le Carré described in *Smiley's People* still stands. Down at the base of the hill there are avenues of lime trees. On certain Sunday mornings the local council organises dog clinics next to the Parliament Hill running track for dogs that have run one lap too many.

Lexington ran up to a rather elegant man in an immaculate three-piece pinstripe grey suit who was flying a royal blue kite. He was not at all pleased – the first sign of displeasure of the morning. An elderly lady carrying a dachshund of equal vintage struggled up to the top of the hill where a man with a dog was hammering in a sign that read, 'LOST READING GLASSES. RING 435 4567.'

I stopped on the crest of the hill. This was familiar territory for both the dogs as we'd been here often before. Lib and Lex sniffed about as if looking for the lost glasses and Julia and I watched the kite-flyers. There is a slightly mad compulsion that drives sensible people to fly kites. Julia's brother-in-law lives near by and is one of those compulsives. He once flew his kite so high from Parliament Hill that he received a written warning from the Department of Transport that he was a hazard to air navigation.

Julia commented that our playful dogs looked like naughty St Trinian's girls and as she spoke a lady with a German shepherd and a miniature wire-haired dachshund crested the hill. She was an attractive woman, so, using her dogs as an excuse for conversation, I asked her, 'Who's the boss?'

'The dach!' she replied. 'He's a monster.' But she was on a dedicated dog-walk and didn't stop to talk.

Soon, a lumbering black Labrador approached and headed straight for our lascivious twosome. His tail was raised, his hair on end and he ambled towards them with the arrogant walk that signals that the guys have arrived. Liberty is quite good in these situations and turns amour into a game, while Lexington is still in awe of manly displays.

As the Labrador sniffed my dogs, a Dalmatian charged up to him, sniffed his bum and tried to mount him.

'He must be a castrate,' said the Dalmatian's nonplussed owner, who by now was beside us. 'Henry is bent. He only fancies castrates.' The Labrador's owner arrived and confirmed the state of affairs.

Parliament Hill was filling with prams, so we re-formed our pack at the spot where Oliver Cromwell regrouped his forces after Charles I dissolved Parliament, descended the hill and headed for the **Hampstead Ponds**. Hampstead itself was probably a Saxon homestead, but in the Domesday Book it had passed to Ranulph Pevrel, who married William the Conqueror's discarded mistress. This is a tradition that in fact is still carried on in Hampstead today, with flats on the side roads leading to the Heath known locally as alimony flats. The wives, with rare exception, get custody of the dogs.

With so many ponds concentrated in such a small area, it's hard to believe that not long ago there were similar ponds throughout London. In fact, in the last hundred years London has lost over ninety per cent of her ponds. The Westbourne and Fleet rivers, now only conduits under London, remembered only by the streets to which they lent their names, both start from these ponds, and until the nineteenth century the West End received its water supply from here. Three dogs, all with wet sticks in their mouths marched past, eyes straight ahead. This stick-collecting is serious business.

As my dogs trotted down towards the ponds, a lecherous dachshund emerged centipede-like from the underbrush and gave chase to Lexington. Lexy went coy and rebuffed his advances while Liberty attempted to step on his head. She was only trying to convince him to play, but with sex on his mind he was not amused.

Julia went to Lexy's assistance and we continued. As we neared the first two ponds, Lexington found high gear once more and launched herself into the water. Where do these dogs find their energy? The boys fishing were not amused, nor was the moorhen with her late chicks. Lex avoided the birds and fish hooks while Lib wallowed in the shallows and dug the mud. These ponds don't hold a candle to the Highgate Ponds only minutes away, for, by late summer they are the colour of French Canadian pea soup, and probably the same consistency and taste.

The dogs emerged from the water without Julia's demand for them to do so, a sure sign that after two hours they were flagging. The two humans were surprised at how fresh we both felt, so instead of heading out of the Heath we detoured up to the **Vale of Health**.

The Vale of Health; what a magnificent name. Percy Bysshe Shelley sailed paper boats on the Vale of Health pond when he was a boy but by the time the area was developed in Victoria's reign it had primarily become a receptacle for dead dogs. Even so, it remained a source of water for the Hampstead Water Company's supplies to the West End until it was closed down as a public health hazard. This part of the park is covered with unnatural hills and troughs which came about when it was excavated for sand and gravel in the nineteenth century. Blackberries grow in abundance, although, as in all of London's parkland, you should never eat berries that grow close to the ground – what with all the long-legged dogs about.

Sigmund Freud's London dog certainly wouldn't have been a hazard. When Freud lived in nearby Maresfield Gardens, and awaited the arrival from quarantine of his 'co-analyst', his chow that attended most of his analytical sessions back in Vienna, he acquired a Pekinese. His family may well have brought it here for exercise, as this is the part of the Heath nearest to old Hampstead.

The traffic noise from West Heath Road and Heath Street reached a crescendo as we approached **Whitestone Pond**, the highest point in London and now a concrete-lined tub floating like a liquid island in a circle of roads. It was not always like this, for Kate Greenaway wrote of a brush her dog Rover once had with two belligerent swans in the pond. There are swans no more, only remote control power boats. Simon Jenkins, the journalist, says that there was once a dog cemetery by the pond, so I set about looking for it. All I found was an old milestone that read, 'IV miles from St Giles Pound & 4½ miles, 29 yards from Holborn Bars'.

As traffic was chaotic and it was now pub opening time, we decided to give the West Heath a miss and make for **The Freemasons Arms** on Downshire Hill.

The dogs were let off their leads once more as we descended back on to the Heath and recommenced their diligent search for whatever dogs diligently search for. It was now almost noon, a brilliantly sunny day cooled by a fresh and gentle late September breeze. As we retraced our steps I recognised the elderly lady whom we had seen carrying her dachshund up Parliament Hill, now carrying her dog back towards the parking lot at the base of the hill, the site used for Hampstead Heath's biannual fun fairs.

Our paths converged and I nodded a 'hello'.

'Have you been carrying him since I saw you on Parliament Hill?' I queried.

'Oh no. He's had his little exercise. I only carry him there and back.'

The dog looked forlorn and embarrassed, as only dogs can look.

'That's an awfully long way for you to carry such a heavy dog for his exercise,' Julia interjected. 'Would you like my husband to carry him for you?'

'Are you kidding?' I thought. The old goat would probably rather die than have me carry him.

'Oh, that's very kind of you to offer,' she replied, 'but I'm quite used to this. I carry him here whenever it's a pleasant day.'

From the cloudiness of his lenses I guessed the dog to be over fifteen years old and when I asked his owner she replied that he was eighteen. That's a magnificent age for any dog, although not wholly unexpected for a dachshund. If dachshunds survive the tribulations of the back problems they suffer from being dwarfs, they are long-lived creatures.

'Why do you take him all the way to Parliament Hill?' I asked.

The elderly owner told me that it wasn't too far, as she only lived in Keats Grove, just outside the Heath entrance. 'This was really my late husband's dog,' she said. 'He was an inveterate kite-flyer. In his youth Fritz used to run like the wind over the Heath while my husband would fly his kite from the hill. It's hard to imagine, looking at him now, that he was once master of the hill.'

I looked at Fritz, glassy-eyed, drawn and thin-skinned, carried like the senile geriatric invalid that he now was and wondered, not for the first time, about the morality of keeping elderly pets alive until they die naturally or deteriorate to such a dramatic degree that their owners ask for them to be put down. Is there any life for an old canine soldier like this?

'There is nothing Fritzy enjoys more than the feeling of the wind on his face,' continued his owner. 'That's why I take him up to the top of the hill where there's always a breeze. I put him down and he has a wee sniff about, then he sits down, just like a seagull does, facing the wind, closes his eyes and smiles. He'd sit there for hours if I'd let him but I'm having guests for lunch so he's only had a short walk today.'

Fritz hadn't had a walk at all. He'd had a carry. Fritz's owner had had the short walk, but I understood exactly what she meant when she said that he closed his eyes and smiled into the wind. The Western mind doesn't credit animals with the ability to think and reason. Most of us feel that animals act only out of instinct or through conditioned response. Even a goodly number of vets, one in four to be precise, fall into this trap of assuming that only humans are aware of their own identities. Our attitude is conditioned by our culture. In Japan, on the other hand, it is unlikely that you will find a single vet – surveys certainly haven't – who denies sentience to other animals.

When Fritz's owner told me that Fritz closed his eyes and smiled, I believed her, not in the direct sense that he was actually smiling but in the indirect sense that a knowing dog-owner through eighteen years of living with an animate creature comes to understand innately the signs of contentment and well-being in her pet. Sitting on Parliament Hill with the breeze blowing in his face undoubtedly stirred in old Fritz's withered body a feeling of what modern medicine, in its desire to obliterate jargon, calls 'wellness'. It was undoubtedly prolonging his life.

I hadn't realised we had been talking for so long and suddenly found myself at the parking lot next to the Heath. Julia looked like a crushed puppy. One day these young dogs of ours will be like old Fritz – we've been through it before with our previous dog. Blissfully unaware, Lib and Lex were called to heel, their leads were put on and we made our exit from the Heath under the row of whispering weeping willows on to Downshire Hill and The Freemasons Arms.

We arrived in time to have our pick of the tables in the large garden and kept the dogs on their leads, knowing that over the next half-hour the garden would fill with many others of diverse size and vintage. Already two St Bernards were patrolling the perimeter, disregarding the neatly painted signs, 'Please keep children and animals off the flower beds'. I assumed these were the landlord's dogs exercising their *droit de seigneur*. They left us alone.

As the dogs had drunk half the pond water on the Heath, there was no need to ask for a bowl of water for them. Julia had a glass of soda water while I had a pint of bitter. I hate bitter! For the eighteen years I've been in England I've tried to develop a taste for the stuff and I'm still persevering. A crispy cold lager is the right drink for a refreshingly sunny day but, like a fool, I'm still trying to find out why the natives drink so much of their home brew.

Sitting in the garden, I looked back at the pub itself and thought that it might well be that from his home above the pub the landlord could look down on the garden of John Keats' home on Keats Grove, where the poet wrote 'Ode to a Nightingale'. At high school in Toronto I was obliged to memorise that ode and hated it as much as I still hate bitter, because it was so alien, so foreign to life as I knew it, but here, sitting under such a blue sky, listening to the birds, I felt compelled to read it again when I got home. Is it living in London for eighteen years or simply advancing years that has done this?

While the dogs rested under the table, I walked over and inspected the thirty-foot-circular, now paved site of what had been the last remaining pell mell court in England. The game pell mell originated in Italy – *palla a maglio*, ball to mallet – and, after becoming the gentleman's sport in France, was introduced into Britain at the same level of the society in the seventeenth century. King Charles II used to play what in English became known as pall mall with his mistresses in St James's Park, but The Freemasons Arms court is the only one that still survives, more or less.

Julia roused the dogs, who happily bounced to attention. Lexington came over for a quick tickle. She's a dog who has a great innate need of contact comfort. Julia, seeing that tickles were being handed out, lined herself up behind Lexington. We departed and walked up the right-hand side of Downshire Hill, past the elegant Regency villas that I would commit larceny for. These homes are wonderful, not only for their elegant proportions and large front and back gardens, but also for their individuality and their proximity to the Heath. The very first house beside The

Freemasons Arms had a massive buddleia growing in its front garden which was smothered in butterflies. Halfway up the hill, on the left-hand side, is the most user-friendly church in London, St John's, Downshire Hill. With its neat porch and balanced windows, it could be transplanted to New England and not seem out of place.

Heavy traffic steamed past on **Hampstead High Street** as we crossed and avoided that main thoroughfare by continuing on to **Thurlow Road**, then left at **Eldon Grove** and right into **Lyndhurst Road**. All of these streets have grass verges, ideal for dogs, and are lined with lime trees, the dirtiest of London's trees. Limes themselves aren't dirty, but they attract myriads of aphids which deposit their discharge on the parked cars below. It's like epoxy resin and, once attacked, cars have been known to be glued in position until dislodged by earthquakes.

Having run the lime gauntlet, we turned into **Lyndhurst Gardens**, which was a pleasure if only because this street is lined with plane trees. The plane loves London but I can't find a place in my heart for it. True, the annual shedding of pieces of bark can give the trunk and main branches a pleasantly mottled appearance, but its autumn leaves are lifeless, a bore, a waste. The dogs started intensively sniffing, disregarding a black and tan mutt that was discreetly attending to his toilet in the gutter. This was old territory for the dogs and for us as our daughters have for the last twelve years attended a nearby school, and for every school day of their lives Liberty and Lexington have come with Julia to pick up or drop off the children.

We walked past a house on the street that had once been part of the school and on to the sharp bend in the road when Julia asked, 'I wonder what became of Miss Hibbert's dogs?'

Miss Hibbert was ninety-one years old when I first met her in 1970, living as a spritely recluse in the grand redbrick Victorian house in which she had been born. I met Miss Hibbert and her cocker spaniels and feral cats when I went on a house visit to her. Although she was arthritic and hard of hearing, her brain was lucid and I could hardly wait to tell Julia of the day's stories about the Hampstead turn-of-the-century set after a visit to this wonderful *grand dame*. It was only a short time before Julia accompanied me on a call. Julia was equally enchanted by Miss Hibbert, but appalled by the state of the rooms in which she lived and thereafter returned with vacuum cleaner and duster to tidy up. This was before our youngest children were born, at a time when Julia was appearing frequently on the stage in the West End and had been nominated for three years in succession as Best Actress of the Year, but Miss Hibbert never knew the other side of her charlady's life.

It was through visiting Miss Hibbert that we heard of the school behind her house, St Christopher's.

The dogs didn't enjoy **Belsize Crescent** and nor did I. This street has been a builders' tip ever since I first saw it and I doubt it will ever be anything else. The display of cacti in the window of Arrival Clothing at the bottom of the street, however, is attractive. I walked across **Belsize Terrace** and past the first veterinary surgery on our route. Belsize was at one time a submanor of Hampstead, but eventually came into the ownership of the Westminster monks who in turn sublet it in the early 1700s to a wealthy coal merchant who built a chapel here where marriages cost only five shillings as long as you held your wedding breakfast on his grounds. This was the beginning of the Belsize pleasure garden, the forerunner of the more famous pleasure gardens at Vauxhall, Marylebone and Ranelagh. An entertainer named Howell ran the pleasure gardens until they closed in 1740, but my dogs were not interested in all of this so we continued marching along. At the bottom of the square, the pavement looked as if someone had dropped a quart of raspberries, but upon looking up Julia saw that they were growing on a tree, a giant raspberry tree! Birds weren't eating the fruit so I picked some leaves and berries and pocketed them to find out what it was later.

If Belsize Crescent is a construction site, **Belsize Park Gardens** is the supply depot. Julia told me that she knows of several recently separated husbands who have flats here but I didn't ask her *how* she knows, and we continued down the road. All the trees are in low-walled gardens. There is nowhere for a dog to do what a dog's got to do. This street too is in the process of being recycled. There were more builders' skips than cars parked along the route.

At **Englands Lane** the street name changes to **Primrose Hill Road** and at the first intersection we all paused while a driver tried to restart her stalled car as her springer spaniel lashed her with a torrent of verbal abuse from the back seat. We continued on to **Primrose Hill**, the end of the first part of our journey.

With military-like precision, I had planned our walk in detail and had Julia leave her car here earlier. Only now she realised that she had left her car keys in my car at Ken Wood. She hailed a passing

17

taxi and told me she'd be back in twenty minutes, while I walked on to Primrose Hill where I lay down on the grass, not too far from a lady who was sitting topless on a sun chair reading Danielle Steel. Her rough collie was sleeping in the shade of a nearby tree but I forbade my dogs to leave my side lest they rent the enchanting tranquillity of the view.

# 𝕎alk 𝕋wo

## Primrose Hill to Hyde Park

START: Elsworthy Road entrance to Primrose Hill, NW3.

END: Cumberland Gate entrance to Hyde Park at Marble Arch, W1.

LENGTH: Approximately 7 miles.

TIME: Approximately 3½ hours.

LEADS: Required in all ornamental garden sections of Regent's Park and in Paddington Gardens.

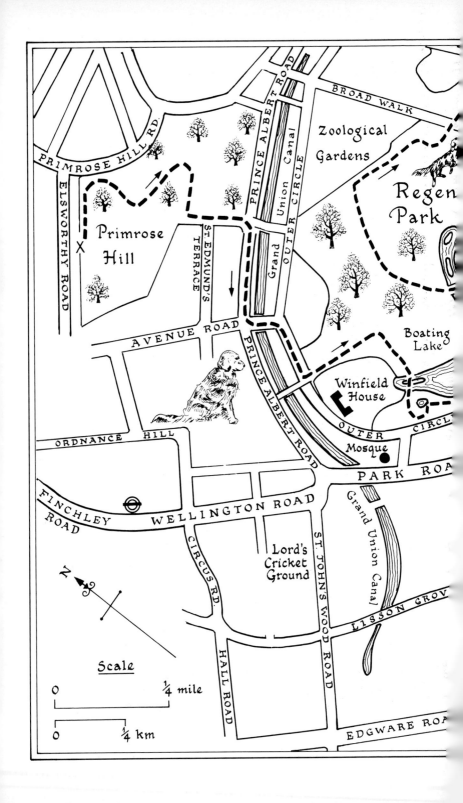

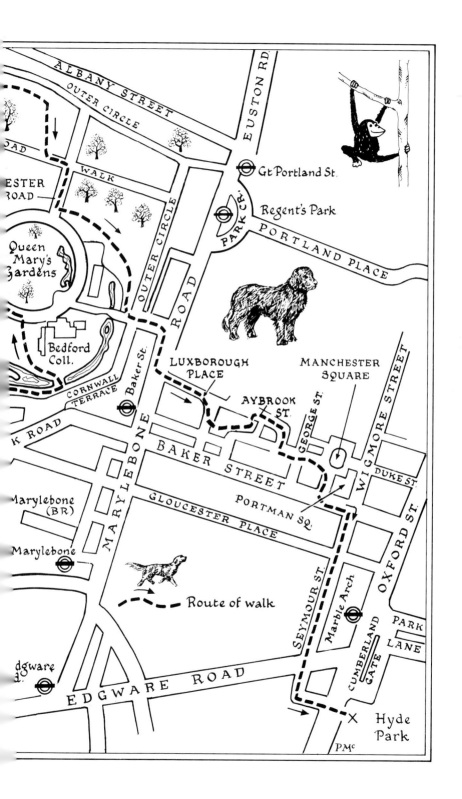

ALBANY STREET

OUTER CIRCLE

WALK

ESTER
ROAD

OAD

Queen
Mary's
Gardens

Bedford
Coll.

CORNWALL
TERRACE

OUTER CIRCLE

OUTER CIRCLE

ROAD

EUSTON RD.

PARK CR.

⊖ Gt Portland St.

Regent's Park

PORTLAND PLACE

LUXBOROUGH
PLACE

MANCHESTER
SQUARE

AYBROOK
ST.

Baker St.

⊖

MARYLEBONE

BAKER

STREET

GEORGE ST.

WIGMORE STREET

DUKE ST.

K ROAD

Marylebone
(BR)

⊖ Marylebone

GLOUCESTER PLACE

PORTMAN SQ.

OXFORD ST.

Route of walk

SEYMOUR ST.

Marble Arch

⊖

CUMBERLAND
GATE

PARK

LANE

dgware
d.

⊖

EDGWARE    ROAD

Hyde
Park

PMc

## From Primrose Hill via Regent's Park and Marylebone to Hyde Park.

**Primrose Hill** is technically part of Regent's Park. It was once simply the highest area of Marylebone Park, King Henry VIII's hunting ground, but in time came into the hands of Eton College. In 1841 the Crown exchanged with Eton College this patch for some of its land near Windsor, and that's why there are dogs here today rather than pupils.

The hill was denuded of trees even before Henry VIII enparked it. It's quite likely that Elizabethan dogs once cavorted on this open space but it has taken three hundred years for it to become the most socially acceptable venue for dog-walking in north London.

There was a redolent and heavy autumn morning mist on the hill, a blanket into which Liberty and Lexington were readily absorbed, as we started off from the Elsworthy Road entrance to the park. The dogs, like greyhounds released from their traps, tore hare-like into the mist. As Julia and I walked along the northern perimeter the noises of a weekday morning, of the traffic on nearby Primrose Hill Road became muffled and disappeared and we were left in a stillness, broken only by the chirrup of sparrows and the plaintive cries of 'Henry!' and 'Sam!' echoing from the fog.

Dogs loomed out of the mist, only to disappear into it again, and Julia and I joined in the morning chorus. 'Liberty! Lexington!' Our twosome emerged from the opalescence grinning with delight at what they had discovered, a canine quorum. At nine o'clock on a weekday morning, Primrose Hill is quite simply riddled with dogs and dog-owners receiving their early morning exercise, and both Sam and Henry had joined our two, nose to tail.

Lex and Lib indulged in skittish early morning behaviour. They danced and teased and pretended they were Formula One racing cars while Julia and I continued walking. Out of the mist ahead of us ambled an elderly golden retriever, a female by the shape of her head and at least ten years old judging from the white hair around her eyes and muzzle and the shuffle in her walk. There is a dignity to old dogs that I quite admire, but as I talked with her guardian who hovered near by I learned that the slow walk was not induced by old age but rather by incipient blindness.

'I found her wandering lost in Camden Town over two years ago,' commented the owner, a sympathetic-looking woman in her early forties. 'I advertised everywhere but no one claimed her, so she joined my menagerie.'

Her menagerie consisted of two equally elderly black and white Battersea Dogs' Home rejects, both of whom also now emerged from the thinning mist. This was obviously a nice lady! I bent down to stroke the old golden and take a surreptitious look at her cataracts just to see how advanced her incipient blindness was.

'I'm sorry. He can't help it,' explained Julia. 'My husband's a vet.'

I didn't mind that she had said so because I was interested in the old dog. Some types of blindness can be corrected with surgery relatively easily, but unfortunately this dog undoubtedly had a hereditary development of both cataracts and retinal atrophy, a condition for which nothing can be done.

'I know you'll disapprove, but I'm treating her herbally,' the owner continued. 'A veterinary surgeon from Scotland is providing her with herbal remedies and she's a little better on them.'

'Mr Rohrbach probably knows more about herbal veterinary medicine than anyone else in the country,' I replied, then answered her forthcoming question by telling her that I had known John for eighteen years. We know an infinitesimal amount about the thera-peutic values of plants and herbal therapy can indeed sometimes be therapeutic. I didn't disapprove at all.

While we were talking, eight dogs including mine had formed a large furry moving circle, noses to tails, and were going in a clockwise direction. Julia shouted at ours who, on command, broke rank and rejoined us. Liberty was slobbering with delight as we proceeded southwards up the hill towards the highest point near central London, 214 feet above sea level.

'The Hill' is simply that, an isolated mound of sand sitting alone on a base of London clay. Primroses must obviously have once proliferated but that was hundreds of years ago. Some were secretly planted again in remote areas of the park a few years back but none of these have survived. We nodded to passing dog-walkers, noticing that this is a women's dog-walking territory. Ken Wood and Hampstead Heath were peopled with males and females equally, but here all of the minders were ladies.

As we neared the summit, I heard a more guttural command: 'Bess. Come here.' It emanated from a male dog-walker, the only one beside myself in the ever-thinning mist of the day, and he was calling either his golden retriever or the young girl who was scampering about with equal abandon.

'I'm usually here at eight in the evening', he said as he eyed and instantly recognised Julia and continued enigmatically, 'but I'm taking my daughter down to Kent today.'

Bess was his dog, the fourth golden we had seen this morning. There was no way of guessing how many others were lurking in the distant recesses of the hill; they were certainly the most prevalent purebreds we had seen so far, outnumbered only by mutts. Bess's name fitted what was becoming a cardinal requirement for dog-walking here. There are no Whiskys, Micks or Dollys walked on Primrose Hill, only Megans, Henrys and Besses, or poseurs like Liberty and Lexington. Primrose Hill caters for a specific class of dogs and dog-walkers. I wondered whether it was any different less than one hundred years ago when Friedrich Engels lived on the eastern side of the hill.

'There are golden retrievers and then there are the others,' offered Bess's owner as we stopped to watch our respective blondes introduce themselves to each other. As the dogs continued their nasal introductions, we continued our verbal one.

'Marvellous with children, obedient, gentle and loving – they're not really dogs, they're golden retrievers.' Here was a man after Julia's heart; someone who intuitively knew how to bowl a female golden retriever owner off her small but perfectly symmetrical feet.

'I must admit, it's about the best breed I know,' I countered and he replied, 'Canadian?'

This man was an observant linguist too. I had uttered the vowel sound that differentiates Americans from Canadians: about – house – mouse. Canadians say, 'abuoot – huoose – muoose'. Americans pronounce it 'abaoot – haoose – maoose'.

As we talked the sun finally burst through the mist revealing a veritable dog rally. Four turbo-charged small lean mongrels were speeding around an imaginary racing circuit, a canine Brands Hatch. Bess, Lex and Lib and then Henry, a Labrador, joined in, Liberty throwing herself into the fray with Lexington hanging back, watching and wishing to join but wondering what would happen to her if she did. As the dogs carried on their shenanigans, their owners unwittingly formed a circle like the stones at Avebury Ring, a bemused gallery, all smiling quietly to themselves at the joy their charges were having. This was the silly essence of the exercise and it made us feel as good as the dogs.

I called my dogs to break ranks once more and, as Julia and I stood at the pinnacle of the hill taking in the gloriously pastel panorama of the city before us, the dogs leapt on imaginary toboggans and hurtled themselves down the incline. They enjoyed it so much they climbed back up and lost themselves in a haze of free-falling exhilaration twice more. Primrose Hill is the best place in London for downhill racing canines.

The grass on the south side of the hill had not been cut this year, a pleasant experiment in natural seeding, which created a Sargasso Sea of undulating long silken mauve vegetation, ideal for dogs to play in and for humans to lie in. Already, early in the morning, there was a snoozing male body stoically guarded by two West Highland terriers. *This* was their exercise.

Now, descending the hill westwards, I wanted to show Julia a little oddity, a surprise. Near the western edge of the park there is what appears to be a natural spring emanating from the hill, a ditch of jet black earth and sparkling water surrounded by a miniature forest of succulent lush deep grass. On our way there we passed three ladies with an exceptionally fat black cocker spaniel cross and then a smartly coiffed almost elegant well-groomed Shih Tzu, apparently off on a stroll by itself. 'I bet that dog's owner is sophisticated,' Julia murmured and on the perimeter path we spotted Mrs Shih Tzu in what Julia said was a Kenzo creation worth thirty brand new Shih Tzus.

As we neared the spring, Liberty leapt forward. She smelt water. She smelt mud. She smelt action. 'Where is this spring?' Julia asked and I pointed in the distance to Libby. 'All I see is a black Labrador,' she replied.

Liberty threw herself into 100-yard dashes, then back into the mud. She disappeared from view, then raised her head to ground level, looking straight at us, after which she submerged herself in the mud once more. Lexington, ever the follower, dived in too but preferred to stand demurely in the mud, coating her legs to the knees, while watching Lib act the fool.

'Bruce! This was not a good idea!' the chief pronounced. 'I would not walk here ever. NEVER!'

Liberty raced out of the mud, over to the elegant Shih Tzu and stood on its head while Julia and I both turned away. Lexington just looked quizzical. I quickly took up conversation with the attractive owner of Butch, a handsome golden retriever as dark in colour as the most luxuriant auburn Irish hair and as big as the much larger American golden retriever.

Julian Huxley, when he lived here, once wrote, perhaps after watching Primrose Hill dog-walking, 'To his dog, every man is Napoleon; hence the constant popularity of dogs.' If, however, your dog looks and smells like a sewer, the popularity fades. Julia called Lexington to heel and I collared Lib. We put their leads on and made a premature exit across **Prince Albert Road** towards the lake in Regent's Park.

A canalside walk has been created along the **Grand Union Canal** and so, rather than go directly aross the Outer Circle Road into the park, we decided to take this path. It would take us in the direction of the lake. Julia used to stop near it but much further west to exercise the dogs before picking up the children from school. However, she no longer does this because of Lexington's propensity to see water and to leap in without thinking. One afternoon, during a short rest and recreation stop, Lexington slipped through the fence and down to the canal. People on a passing canal barge shouted to Julia to ask whether she knew whose dog was swimming full steam a few hundred yards up the canal. She quickly grabbed Liberty and raced her back to the car, figuring that she should return home with at least one dog, then sped back to the canal, where the barge had by now backed up, found Lexington and, by calling to her, was drawing her back around the bend to within earshot of her owner. Lexington finally sighted Julia and swam towards her, having now been swimming for almost half an hour. Julia, who was going to a school meeting and was dressed in a delicate red print silk dress, lay down flat on the canal embankment, stretched as far as she could and grabbed Lexington by the scruff, hauling her up the three-foot concrete wall from the water. It was then straight over to me where I pronounced Lexington clinically shocked but otherwise fine. So was my wife, a lady with unexpectedly strong arm muscles!

We crossed Prince Albert Road to the canal, to the obvious enjoyment of the slow traffic. Liberty was covered from the top of her head to the tip of her scraggly tail in a sticky tar-like mud. Lorry-drivers honked their horns, but the chief was not amused.

The canalside walk here at the edge of the Zoo is a path overgrown with brambles and nettles and peopled by winos and meths drinkers. The entire path is littered with a non-stop selection of cider bottles, beer cans and human excrement. It is an unsavoury place, best avoided. We left at the first opportunity, climbing the hill beside **Macclesfield Bridge** at **North Gate** and then crossing over it and into the park. A mature London plane tree grows on the western side of the bridge and as we climbed past it I saw a massive scar thirty feet long on the side facing the canal. This was created over a hundred years ago, in 1874, by a barge carrying explosives which blew up right under the bridge. Windows were blown out miles away and I dare say that if Friedrich Engels was at home that night over at Regent's Park Road, working on his treatise, he would have heard it too.

There were no dogs or people in the park outside the **Outer Circle** and the chief and I walked in the direction of the park entrance beside **Winfield House**, the American Ambassador's residence, while both dogs rolled in the recently cut long grass, removing much of the Primrose Hill residue.

At this entrance to the main part of Regent's Park there is a small stretch of ornamental garden which is fenced off from the footpath. A sign states that dogs should be walked through the area on their leads. The sign does not mention wives, however, and at the sight of the first conker glistening in the grass Julia polevaulted over the fence to the greenery beyond and told me she would catch up with us in a few minutes. I walked the dogs on and then took off their leads. This area of the park is still partly wooded. In 1649, a survey of the area listed 16,297 trees, oak, ash, elm, whitethorn and maple, but virtually all have now been felled, often replaced by horse chestnuts like the one Julia was scavenging under right now. She rejoined us shortly, the pockets of her denim jacket bulging like Harpo Marx's, and we continued walking southwards towards the dog bath, Julia stopping intermittently to utter things such as, 'That was one falling off!' while she perused the landscape looking for yet another fallen nut.

As we approached the bridge that separates the western bird sanctuary from the boating lake, a dishevelled Yorkshire terrier with a raspy bark tried to obliterate Lib as she bent down to say hello. I would have done the same thing if something as filthy and smelly as Liberty came my way, but the owner, whom I recognised as one of my clients, quickly apologised for her dog's behaviour.

'She has an excuse for acting like the little bitch that she is,' the owner said. 'She's just finishing her season. I do wish she would stop pestering me, though. I'm getting tired of her waking me up every hour each night and showing me her bum.' The owner demonstrated her dog's behaviour and passers-by stood and gaped, not quite understanding the open and unselfconscious relationship some clients have with their vet.

'Look! There's a punk duck,' Julia sighed, pointing out a red-crested pochard.

We stopped for a few minutes and contemplated the picture-book serenity of the ducks and geese in their haven, then continued on, wanting to cleanse the dogs as soon as possible. Lexington eyed the boating pool and headed straight for it. She looked, decided that her feet could touch the bottom, and stepped in, realising only as she hit the water that it was much deeper than she had expected. I guess this is what she had done in the Grand Union Canal with Julia. I went over, grabbed her scruff and pulled her out, whereby she shook herself and intentionally fell in again. She swam like a duck, the Mark Spitz of her species, as Liberty raced back and forth at the edge, desperate to join her but without the self-confidence to do so.

I hauled her out once more and headed both of them past the many men carrying chain leads and on towards the lake. With the more gentle incline of the lake embankment, Lib was willing to enter the water and cleansed the lower part of her body. Both dogs darted in and out of the water, shaking themselves, sniffing about and then, if it was Lexington, plunging back in, if it was Liberty, wading back in and lying down. The men swinging their heavy chain leads were not amused. Those weren't chain leads they were swinging, either. They were carrying enormous worry beads. We were near the mosque, in a canine no man's land.

There were only two other dogs in sight, a wet Cavalier King Charles spaniel walking in our direction and a heavy Newfoundland patrolling the lake perimeter looking for a child to save. The lake was riddled with birds: masses of gulls perched on the boats moored in the centre of the lake and cavalcades of black and brown tufted ducks doing real duck dives. In the summer, this side of the lake is populated by extended Arab families, groups of veiled women who have a fearful antipathy towards dogs based on their cultural attitude towards an animal that has endemically carried rabies in their home countries. Even fifteen years ago, it was odd for me to treat a dog owned by an Arab family, but attitudes are changing slowly and today it is far less rare; in fact I see perhaps as many Arab clients as Americans.

As we walked along the outside edge of the lake, the dogs weaving in and out of the water, I saw a traffic jam ahead, the morning waddle of over fifty Canada geese from the park lawn, across the path and into the water. Liberty and Lexington were put in good behaviour mode as the procession passed and were then told they could do what they wanted. I'd forgotten that, to dogs, goose droppings are like *foie gras* is to some of their owners! Leads were quickly placed on both canines and we quickly marched on to the bridge over the lake at **Clarence Gate**.

Julia delighted in the 'window boxes' of geraniums on the bridge and the ornamental garden on the far side where we turned left and up along the Oregon-ash and weeping-willow-lined lakefront, towards the Inner Circle. An elderly woman with a black Labrador appeared fearful when she saw our dogs, so I put both of ours on their leads.

As we walked on silently past the bandstand, Julia told me she never comes this way because of her memory of the hideous bombing of an army band playing here only a few years ago. The same thought was in my mind. I had been but a short distance away that day, at the American Ambassador's residence, when the bombers struck. The Ambassador's cairn terrier had had pups and as I was examining them I heard the explosion. No one at Winfield House took much notice of the noise, but I had heard bombs before and knew exactly what it was, though not who or what had been attacked.

As I left the park, emergency services vehicles poured in. Later that day I had to return, this time with special permission to pass the police lines. The cairn terrier had taken a dislike to so many people coming in to see her and her litter and had done what any sensible dog would do. One by one, she had taken her pups outside and down into the safety of a rabbit warren at the far end of the garden. While I was helping to dig the pups out of their secure underground shelter, ambulance crews only a few hundred yards away were collecting plastic bags full of pieces of men's bodies. Today, the sight is as tranquil and peaceful as one would ever want, but to me the weeping willows are in permanent mourning.

It was in a sombre mood that we reached the **Inner Circle** and walked past **The Holme**, the most magnificent private residence in London. When the Prince Regent and John Nash created Regent's Park, their plan was to encircle this road with a grand assortment of stucco-iced wedding cake houses. It was, however, too costly an exercise, and the plan was never completed.

Just past The Holme we returned to the park and open parkland.

The mist had by now completely burnt away and it was a brisk refreshing day. We walked towards the bridge over the large bird sanctuary. A well-illustrated sign shows that twenty-four different species of duck and eight species of geese use this sanctuary. It is also where herons nest in mid-winter and hatch their eggs in April. Each day these gawky and gloriously elegant birds take off from their heronry and fly over the traffic of Baker Street and Oxford Street or Bayswater Road to go fishing in Hyde Park or Kensington Gardens.

Julia spied a few more punk ducks and while she pondered over who their hair stylist was, an African pochard came begging towards Lexington. Underneath old 'butter wouldn't melt in her mouth' lurks a real dog. I've seen her lick her lips when my African grey parrot has flown across my lounge. I held Lex by her collar as the pochard investigated her. She showed only inquisitiveness towards her feathered friend and, when the pochard realised that Lex did not have any crusts on her person, it waddled away. Two traffic wardens walked past commenting to each other on how the colour of a moorhen's feet is exactly the same as the colour of a Metropolitan Police vehicle clamp. Julia, in the meantime, was at the other side of the bridge contemplating the water.

'I'm so sorry that Danny Kaye is dead,' she sighed. Now I've lived with this lady for over fifteen years, but her thought processes still catch me out sometimes. I didn't reply, but rather, leaned on the railing and took in the view. Swans! There in the lake were two swans, an elegant Persil-white number and an immature dirty grey feathered young swan. I looked at them and dearly missed Danny Kaye too.

Before us now lay the large open flat expanse of the northern perimeter of Regent's Park. Seagulls and groundsmen were clearing up litter.

'Tap af tha marnin',' said a groundsman in a sliceable accent.

'Tap af tha marnin' to you,' I replied.

There are regional English accents that still give me difficulty, but Irish has never been one of them. In fact, I find it closest to Canadian. Until the park was created, this area was a great source of hay and dairy products for London. It had been so for hundreds of years and in 1748 a Swedish botanist, Pehr Kalm, noted that the fields were cut and the hay stacked by itinerant Irishmen. Our friendly groundsman was perhaps unwittingly carrying on a centuries-old tradition.

In front of us lay nine playing fields and fortunately there were few dogs and owners on them. A black and white cocker, together with a Tibetan terrier and a black mongrel with a gimpy leg, were reluctantly being force-marched by a dedicated female dog-walker while a short distance behind her a lithe black short-haired slinky number was stealing bread from two fat wood pigeons.

An unremitting caa-ing emanated from the plane trees. As the dogs trotted their zig-zags, I watched a bag lady sit down in the middle of a field and there remain still and lifeless. Soon, a crow descended from the trees and it too remained still and motionless. Then another alighted, followed by more. Was this Alfred Hitchcock's ghost returned? Within five minutes, over forty crows had formed a semi-circle. 'They're horrid,' said Julia, but all I could see was Lila Kedrova's death scene in *Zorba the Greek* when the cackling old black-clad ladies gather to share the spoils once Kedrova has died.

Slowly the bag lady moved. Her arm swung slowly back and forth. As we walked closer, we saw that she was feeding her feathered friends.

Carrion crows are now common throughout London, although this has not always been the case. It is only in the last thirty years that they have roosted in such large numbers in the centre of the city. When I first arrived here in 1970, crows didn't roost in significant numbers in Regent's Park, but now these iridescent and admittedly sinister-looking birds are as common as gulls. Three times daily, a woman known locally as the crow lady arrives on her bicycle, laden with balls of bread and other crow goodies. She bicycles through the park like Johnny Appleseed sprinkling apple-seed aross America, spreading her crow morsels, often followed by scavenging Jack Russells looking for a free hand-out – or an unsuspecting crow.

As we continued, another walker passed us, pestered by her own Jack Russell. 'Where's the squirrel? Find the squirrel!' she demanded of her imploring dog. There was a recent unsuccessful attempt to reintroduce red squirrels into Regent's Park, and I now understood why the experiment had failed.

I commanded Lib and Lex to 'heel' as a police motorcycle patrol hummed past, then released them from their command. They darted straight at a Staffordshire bull terrier. The owner grabbed her and lifted her up in his arms. 'I'm so sorry,' Julia implored and he replied that it was quite all right but he didn't want to take any chances. Staffordshire bull terriers were once bred as fighting dogs and, although professional breeders have been marvellous at breeding out any inherent blood lust, these dogs can still be taught to fight, usually through painful and abusive training.

Dog-fighting is on the increase in London. English bull terriers and Staffordshire bull terriers have been crossbred with the American pit bull terriers in an attempt to create a beast with a greater blood lust. It's an entertainment of the unemployed and the bored, very much a back-of-the-warehouse phenomenon. This dog-walker, the owner of Bouncer, had, he told me, come in for quite a lot of trouble.

'I thought it would be safe to walk my dog here,' he continued. 'I used to take her to the Scrubs, but there were too many aggressive dogs there. I've had two men come up to me in the park and offer money for Bouncer to fight. She's not a fighting dog. She's just a pet. One of those men kept following me with his dog and you could tell that his brute was a fighter. I kept telling him to go away but he kept on annoying my dog and I finally had to hit him before he left.'

Poetic, I thought. Someone thinks he's tough and trains his dog to be a fighter, to be a manifestation of his personality. But, in fact, the dog is only the manifestation of what he *wants* to be, not what he really is. Then 'tough guy' meets a tattooed gentle giant with a dog that has been selected and trained to be a house pet and, with nothing more than a forceful shove, he tucks his tail between his legs and barrels out of the park.

Bouncer did however have scars. I could see them. 'How did he get injured?' I asked.

'I was walking with Bouncer just over there,' he said, pointing westwards to the park entrance beside Winfield House, 'when I saw a man about a hundred feet away set his two Staffs on Bouncer. I grabbed the male by its neck and smashed it against a tree twice, as hard as I could, then threw it away, but it came right back and hit Bouncer again. I kicked the female and she limped away, then I kicked the male and picked up Bouncer. The owner watched everything with his hands folded. I rushed off to the vet who patched Bouncer up. She had tears to her ears and neck and got an infected elbow joint. I went to the Parks Police and gave them a description of the man and his dogs. I don't know if they caught him. I've never seen him since, but I'd like to.'

I'll bet he would, and I'd like to be there to see them meet too.

Satisfied that I wasn't going to set my dogs on his, Bouncer's owner dropped her back on the ground and with a parting wave we proceeded in our different directions.

Ahead of us Julia and I could see a panoramic outline of the Zoo. We could hear it too, a cacophony of noise. John Updike, when he lived near Regent's Park, once said that when he heard a growl he didn't know whether it was a lion or his table partner's stomach, but we had no such problem as the four of us approached the outer enclosure. To the right was the elephant pavilion which, because of the park perspective, gave the appearance that the elephants could freely walk from their pavilion across into the park.

I worked at the Zoo in 1970, on a scholarship from Ontario. That work was in fact what drew me to London and, while I was there, I heard unexpected stories of zoo life. The penguin pool, for example, is architecturally a classic model of the school of International Modernism. It is a magnet for students of architecture, but not for penguins. It was built without a complete understanding of penguins' needs and is not deep enough. When the pool was opened, a few penguins, being deep-diving birds, tried it out and ended up with splitting headaches.

As we approached the elephant pavilion, Liberty and Lexington were joined by a fiercely handsome long-limbed Weimaraner who took great delight in investigating both of them. Lexington collapsed and rolled over while Lib went skittish, running tight circles asking him to play. The Weimaraner trotted back to the bench where his young master was sitting, whereupon his owner leapt up and fled. 'You know your dog,' I commented as we both watched the dog pee where the boy had just been sitting.

Lib and Lex ran down the incline to investigate the goats in the children's zoo, leaving Julia and me to contemplate the elephants.

'I've gone off zoos,' she murmured. 'It's not right. I know it's interesting for us but what about them?'

As we watched, a keeper commanded his elephant to lie down. When it had done so, he walked away, then returned with a hard garden broom and proceeded to sweep vigorously first the elephant's head and then its back. The animal was entranced by the feeling. While this grooming was being carried out, another keeper arrived astride a second elephant, which, upon command, lifted her right foreleg to act as a step as the keeper descended.

The Regent's Park Zoo has come a long way since it was first founded by Sir Humphrey Raffles. The original zoological garden

33

concept of Decimus Burton is antiquated today, yet parts of his original plan still exist. When the Zoo first opened, whips had to be left at the gate but ladies still used their parasols to poke animals. We are much more sensitive to the needs of animals today, to their psychological as well as their physical well-being, which is why Julia, and many others, have gone off zoos.

Regent's Park Zoo might ponder dozens of reasons why they operate at such a great financial loss, but an obvious one is staring them in the face. I can't say that I've gone off zoos – not thoughtful, well-planned, large zoos. I haven't gone off humane livestock farming or the conscientious keeping of domestic pets, either. There is naturally a difference between the forced enclosure of domesticated and wild animals, but many of the animals I treated when I worked at the Zoo were domesticated zoo animals: Père David deer, greater kudus, tigers, capuchin monkeys, all bred at this zoo or others. This was their life. They had known no other, just as Lexington and Liberty have been denied the right to form a hunting pack with other dogs and to forage for themselves in a 'natural' way. Animals have rights. But, as the most powerful creatures on earth, we have a responsibility to care for them in as sensible and as humane a way as we can.

As we walked eastwards from the elephant pavilion, I gathered Julia and the dogs around and asked them if they knew what had happened to the zoo animals during the Second World War. When none of them could answer, I explained that the deadlies were killed and the others were eaten. Liberty and Lexington looked disgusted and ran off to investigate a massive white mountain which turned out to be a Pyrenean mountain dog rubbing its ears on the ground.

We had been walking for two and a half hours now and Julia had forgotten her fruit gum rations, so, with food and drink on our minds, we headed to the eastern periphery of the park, past rows of sycamore trees and couples snogging in the grass, then right, paralleling the Outer Circle, and down towards Marylebone Road. This area of the park is open, flat and relatively treeless. A grumpy man walking a black Labrador in a Guide Dogs for the Blind harness skulked past, doing what he obviously disliked or didn't have the time to do, while two Westies chasing a squirrel unceremoniously ran over one of the horizontal couples. I wondered if these were the guard Westies we had seen earlier in the day on Primrose Hill.

While I observed the practised technique of a black and white dog defecating directly on to a tree, Liberty was investigating another black Labrador. This one was ponderous and slow-moving. I knew instantly who it was: Leila, a patient of mine born of aristocratic pedigree in Kabul, Afghanistan, a dog once owned by a maharajah who in her lifetime has climbed mountains in the Hindu Kush and who has now in her advancing years gone totally blind. She had developed a pyometra, a pus-filled womb, and a decision had to be made whether to operate or euthanase in view of her blindness. Her owner Peter Connell, a retired diplomat, had assured me that she was a happy and contented beast who coped exceptionally well with her blindness. Now was the first time I had ever seen her out walking.

I walked over and called a hello to Mr Connell, to which Leila immediately perked up her ears and stared, as it were, in my direction. 'She recognises your voice,' I was assured.

When her owner moved from Kabul to Delhi, Leila had to be illegally transferred out of Afghanistan. There is a prohibition on the export of any dogs that are born in Afghanistan, a law enacted to maintain the stock of native Afghan dogs, although from my experience Afghans aren't the most brilliant dogs in existence, with brains as thick as their coats. Leila's owner agreed. 'I once saw one in Kabul run straight into a tree when it became excited and break its neck.'

We walked along with Leila following, rooting under trees, rolling on whatever took her fancy and actually playing with other dogs that came up to her. I was frankly impressed. My dogs were off looking for more excitement. Peter Connell told me that he had chosen to live here so that Leila would have easy access to flat open space on which to exercise. He knew before he left India that Leila was going blind. 'I had invited my vet in Delhi over for dinner and later, whilst we were watching a film, he saw the reflection of the cataracts in her eyes for the first time.'

By the time Leila had come through quarantine she was almost totally blind.

'I can think of more amenable places in which to live. I'm thinking of Minorca and shall be visiting there shortly, but doubt that I shall leave before Leila goes. It would be unfair to her to put her through another plane journey and then have her learn to find her way around a new home and environment. She enjoys the weather once it gets cooler. She even forces me to turn down the fire in the bedroom in the winter. In Kabul, she could *smell* the first snow of winter before she could actually see it and would launch herself into it and go wild with joy. She loved snow. She was a marvellously active dog. Once, when I was mountain-climbing, I found myself in a difficult spot and actually felt rather frightened. Leila in the meantime was trotting from ledge to ledge, no fear at all, and she soothed my fears and helped me to get back down. Now when I go jogging in the morning, it's twenty steps forward then nineteen back to see how she is.'

Over the years in veterinary practice I have evolved a definition of what I consider to be the minimum requirements that are necessary to maintain the quality of a pet's life. The animal should be able to enjoy eating and drinking, sleep soundly and comfortably, and be able to move around under its own steam and without distress. My previous dog, Honey, went deaf in her advancing years but she learned to respond to visual signals and coped well with this loss. Later on in her great age, her hind limbs lost their strength and this was the determining factor in my putting her to sleep. Blindness in a dog or a cat has always been, to my mind, an overwhelming disability. Sight is, next to scent, the most important sense that a dog has, or at least that's what I have thought for most of my professional life. I've changed my views slightly as I have come to realise that for many dogs, touch is a paramount sense.

Seeing Leila amble along, nonchalantly having a roll, digging under a tree, sniffing other dogs, I could find no reason to justify my feelings that it is only selfishness on the owner's part that keeps blind dogs alive. Leila was a contented and happy dog who had come to terms with her blindness. Her deficit has certainly deepened her owner's relationship with her, as well as complicated his life, but these didn't appear to me to be disadvantages. To know that this blind dignified old dog had once had legs like pistons that propelled her through the Hindu Kush was simply nostalgic. She is a happy dog now and seeing her had been an instructive professional lesson for me.

Leila has a set circuit that she walks each morning and so, leaving her with her owner, Julia and I walked back to the tunnel of beech trees leading to **Chester Road** where we noticed that our shoes were smothered in orange pollen. I checked the dog's feet. They were the same. I have no idea what it had come from. The continuing path across the road leads through ornamental gardens where dogs must be kept on leads, so we turned right towards **St**

**John's Lodge.** Inside the Inner Circle is Queen Mary's Gardens, certainly one of the finest public gardens in London, but no place for a dog, so we turned left into open parkland. Just off the Inner Circle near St John's Lodge there is a sculpture of a little shepherd girl dedicated to all the protectors of the defenceless. This is where lost Yorkies congregate when they have misplaced their mistresses.

The Nash terraces along the eastern side of the park are a visual treat. All the terraces around the park have now been rehabilitated and I dare say they have never looked so good. I'll bet Jane Asher learned how to ice cakes by looking at these façades.

We passed girls from Queen's College, where our eldest daughter once went to school, playing field hockey, and forbade the dogs from participating. A wily-faced small German shepherd cross marched past in a purposeful manner and I recognised him as Strawb, a free-range dog, originally from St James's but now living in Camden. Strawb is a pub dog and when his master transferred from a pub near Victoria on the far side of Hyde Park to another in Camden beyond the top end of Regent's Park, Strawb took to wandering back each day to his old territory. No one knows how he found his way the first time. He simply showed up at the old pub and was returned to his master. He did it again the next day and it is now his daily ritual. When his owner first told me I said that if he didn't keep Strawb under control he'd be dead within months, but here, two years later, he was obviously still very much alive and still up to his old daily routine. My dogs looked on in envy but I told them to not even *think* of doing anything on their own.

Strawb wasn't interested in us, only in his peripatetic adventures, so we continued to **York Gate** and out of the park. As we stood at the traffic light at **Marylebone Road,** or to be more exact, as Julia and I stood and the dogs sat, Julia expleted, 'I hate it!' She has to sit in this traffic daily on school runs.

We crossed over to **Luxborough Street** and walked down towards **Paddington Gardens** on **Paddington Street**. Luxborough Street has masses of green open space but it is all signposted 'No Dogs Allowed'. This has always been the case. In 1791 this area around York Gate was weekend cottage country for affluent Londoners, one of whom prized his privacy sufficiently to put up a sign reading, 'Steel traps all over these grounds. N.B. Dogs trespassing will be shot.' He would undoubtedly have had more than his fair share of revellers to contend with, for the area we were

37

approaching was until 1778 the Marylebone Gardens, an entertainment gardens where dog fights were held. Paddington Gardens today is on the site of St George's burial grounds and is primarily frequented by secretaries on lunch breaks. Dogs must be walked on leads, and it is the first place in London where I have seen special red receptacles for dog dirt. At least the City of Westminster is doing something constructive to control dog mess by providing receptacles for its removal.

We left the gardens at the **Moxon Street** entrance and stopped at **The Bricklayers Arms** on **Aybrook Street** for a quick drink for us and the dogs. From our seats outside the pub, we had a view of the derelict wasteland that has been a temporary car park, possibly since the Second World War, which is also the largest unknown nature reserve in the West End. In 1975, a local inhabitant rhetorically asked herself if wild flowers still grew anywhere in the West End. What Rosalind Hadden discovered amazed her. She found 155 different species of plants growing wild in the West End and over fifty of these were here in this car park. Nettles, dock, elder, willow, bittersweet, bracken, burdock, buttercups, daisies and yarrow, thistle and buddleia – they were all here, and with them bees and butterflies and insects. She found a treasure trove of nature. We sat and mused at what lay before us then turned right on **Blandford Street** past the Dorothy Parker graffiti and left down **Manchester Street** towards **Manchester Square**. This is uneventful London if you're dog-walking except for the highly poisonous tropical thorn-apple that Mrs Hadden found lurking demurely behind a railing in Manchester Square.

From Manchester Square we walked around **Portman Square**, a private three acres where Liberty was first trained when I lived near by. The traffic noise from Baker Street was, as always, deafening, and it was hard to visualise a time when this land was rural, but rural it once was. In the 1750s this had been cattle-grazing land farmed by Anne Berry. When rinderpest wiped out her herd she was compensated forty shillings for each cow. Less than forty years later, it had all been developed as a speculative real-estate venture. The house in which I lived and practised for fourteen years, at 22 Seymour Street, was standing and occupied. We walked past and all, with the exception of Lexington, who didn't know any better, uttered sighs of nostalgia.

Now we were on a route that I had walked perhaps ten thousand times, along **Seymour Street**, across **Edgware Road**, through the bottom of **Connaught Square**, down **Stanhope Place** to the crosswalk across the **Bayswater Road** and then into **Hyde Park**. I had walked that route mainly with our previous golden retriever, Honey. Most of us have an extra special dog in our lifetimes and she was it. A sensible and reliable being, she spent her summers lying on the pavement on Seymour Street outside our house and the winters curled up on a chair in my reception room watching the comings and goings of her brethren. She always walked without a lead on the route I was now taking my two other dogs. She was a sensible dog who always stopped at roads and waited for permission to cross.

Liberty is moderately vacuous and will never be as reliable, although Lexington has it in her to become as conscientious as Honey was. Lexington, however, is led by the flake and, as we entered Hyde Park, Liberty tugged at her lead, imploring me to release her. She knew that the Serpentine was only a short distance away, but both dogs remained bound to their owners.

It had been a fun morning. This is the part of London I know best yet, even so, it had been a refreshing, even informative, walk. Although we all felt that we could happily carry on, I was reluctant to do so for a simple medical reason. I had spayed Liberty only ten days before and knew that she had had enough exercise for the day.

# 𝔚𝔞𝔩𝔨 𝔗𝔥𝔯𝔢𝔢

## Regent's Park to St James's Park

START: Clarence Gate
(Baker Street) entrance to
Regent's Park, NW1.

END: Carlton Terrace entrance
to St James's Park by
Admiralty Arch, SW1.

LENGTH: Approximately 6 miles.

TIME: Approximately 3 hours.

LEADS: Required in all
gardens and squares. Dogs are
not allowed in either Gordon
Square or St James's Square.

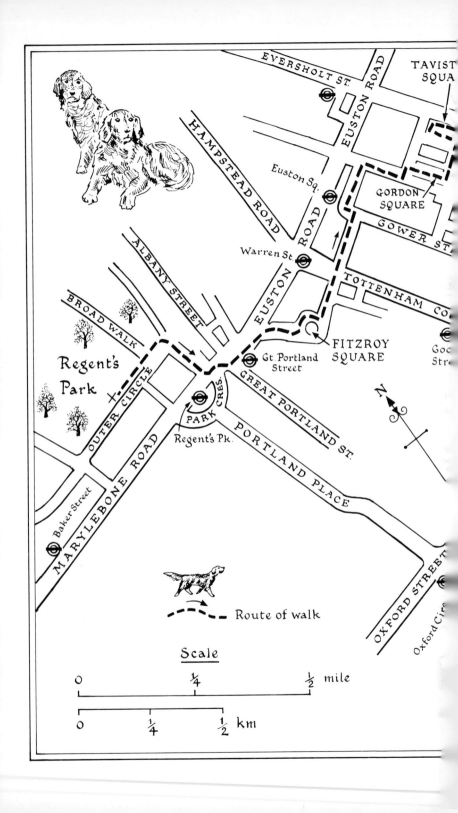

Route of walk

### Scale

0      ¼      ½ mile

0      ¼      ½ km

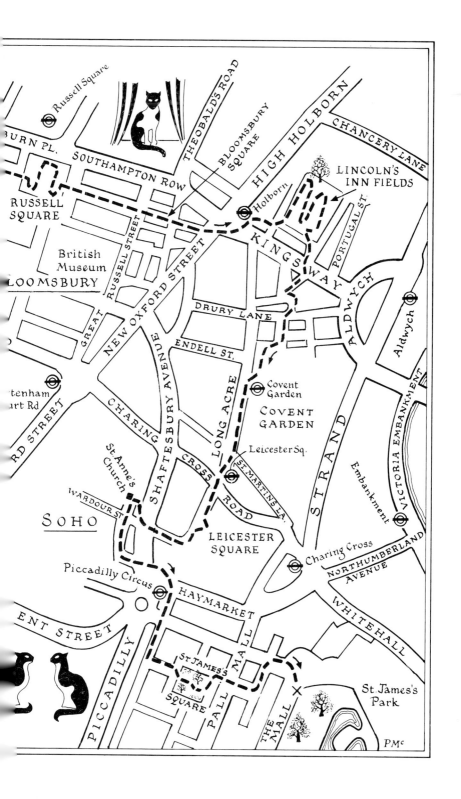

**The first section of a two-part 'dog leg' from Regent's Park, through Bloomsbury, Covent Garden and Soho, to St James's Park**

People are often amazed when they discover that I practise veterinary medicine in W1, in the West End of London.

'Surely people don't keep dogs there,' I've been told countless times. 'Where can they possibly exercise their dogs!'

Although large parts of Bloomsbury, Covent Garden and Soho are indeed commercial, there is still a surprisingly large and settled residential population and, as sure as there are families, dogs follow. What's more, because these inner regions of London were, in another era, far more residential than they now are – middle-class areas – there are excellent facilities for exercising dogs: the historic squares, churchyards and Lincoln's Inn Fields. There really are dogs here, and that's one of the reasons for making this dog leg. The other is that it goes through parts of London that essentially haven't changed over the years. Bloomsbury is like the land that time forgot, although Covent Garden is substantially more than a recycled flower, fruit and vegetable market.

Under an overcast sky and with rain threatening, Julia and I and the dogs entered **Regent's Park** at the Baker Street access. A pirate immediately sauntered past – a black and white ruffian, a muscle-bound street urchin with a bold black patch of hair round his left eye.

'Bet you call him Patch,' I ventured to the owner, thinking that was a safe opener.

'Now, Dr Fogle,' came the rather stern reply, 'you know as well as I that his name is Chuck. Shouldn't you be at work?'

Whoops! She was right. It was a weekday and I was on my own patch. I'm the only vet from the West End clear through to the other side of the City. And not at work!

I wanted both our dogs to burn up some energy here in Regent's Park before tethering them for the walk through public squares and gardens of Bloomsbury. Lexington obliged almost immediately with a fall into the lake, which she did with the aplomb of Rowan Atkinson walking into a lamp post. With her eyes riveted upon us and cruising at good speed, she suddenly discovered that there was no pavement under her limbs and sank. Liberty floundered on the edge and Julia cursed. She hadn't anticipated having to bath the dogs yet again.

The early-morning dog-walkers were everywhere but I didn't say a word to any of them. I wasn't going to run the risk of offending another one of my clients. Cocker spaniels predominated, mostly walked by men, but Liberty and Lexington were too interested in playing leapfrog back and forth over the low fence that separates the footpath from the canal-like extension of the boating lake to notice.

'Love your dogs. Are they Labradors?' A couple from Montreal were snapping photos of my soaking canines. 'You're so lucky here having so much space. We'd love to have a dog but there isn't anywhere in Montreal where we could let a dog run free.'

Julia grinned. She was thinking what I was thinking. North Americans just *luv* London. These folks loved it so much they had conveniently forgotten that Montreal has a *mountain* smack dab in the middle of the city where you can walk your dog!

'Look at the Shih Tzu,' Julia said as we continued towards the Great Portland Street exit. 'Her collar is exactly the same colour as her owner's belt and ear rings.'

'That's a Lhasa Apso,' I replied.

'It's a Shih Tzu!' countered the commander-in-chief.

There are, on occasion, reasonable causes for arguments but this was not one of them. I nodded, and turned sideways to avoid being knocked over by the 'Shih Tzu' owner's flying buttresses of shoulder pads and continued on through the lingering cloud of Ralph Lauren perfume she had left behind.

The dogs were now more interested in canine happenings and went off to explore a fat Labrador's bum. The sky was black and the air still. I muttered to Julia that it might rain any minute but she didn't reply. She wasn't there.

'Where am I?' I heard from the distance.

The dogs ceased their anal investigations, snapped to attention and looked for the source of the voice. Nine fifteen in the morning, it's about to rain and Julia is off playing hide-and-seek! I wasn't in the mood. Dull weather makes me feel dull and this was a classic dull November-like day, although it was still early October. Julia on the other hand revels in wet misty weather. It makes her feel secure and cosy and wanting to play hide-and-seek!

'I'm in the hiding tree,' she shouted.

The dogs apparently understood this, for they immediately

rushed under a drooping ornamental and dragged her out from under it.

'Are they bitches?' a passing man with a collie-type dog asked, and I muttered, 'Yes.'

We passed the Broad Walk, still in lush bloom, directed the dogs to keep to the right to avoid their coming near the flower beds and approached the **Park Square** exit. An elderly and concerned-looking lady was awaiting with her exorbitantly grotesque rotund mongrel. 'Take care. Are they bitches? My Sally hates bitches.' Before I could react, Liberty was at Sally's fore investigating what she had had for breakfast and Lexington was at her aft investigating what she had eaten the day before. Sally looked perplexed then dropped down on her forelegs into a play position.

'Why I never!' beamed her owner. 'Sally never plays with bitches.'

Sally was self-evidently a spayed bitch, a dog that had gone to fat after she had been neutered. She was eight years old.

'Have you ever tried to get that weight off her?' I asked.

'Oh, I'm trying all the time but when she looks at me with those big mournful eyes I just give in. I eat all my meals in my loo now or she sees me and makes me share my meal with her.'

Julia said nothing. She knew as well as I that nothing would change Sally's owner's ways. The misguided love was too deep.

The traffic on Marylebone Road was as chaotic as ever as we put the dogs on their leads, crossed the road, walked past the **Great Portland Street** Underground Station, turned on to **Warren Street** and entered Bloomsbury. The noise died away as we entered the sympathetically pedestrianised **Fitzroy Square**.

The gardens are private, but a black and white cat, unseen by the dogs, slid across the cobbles and into it. The quiet, simple elegance of the buildings give a feeling of timelessness. The south and east sides of the square, originally designed by the Adam brothers, are partly hidden by the massive plane trees. The hospital for the clergy on the north side evokes another era, an anachronism in the London of the late 1980s. When Bette Midler was once asked about the time difference between London and New York she replied. 'When it's three o'clock in New York, it's still 1938 in London.' That's how it feels here.

'That's where Virginia Woolf lived,' whispered Julia pointing to number 29.

I was impressed! I knew she was a Woolf addict but I didn't know she knew such trivia.

'Shaw lived there too, but not at the same time,' I replied at once, proving that I too knew my trivia and would not be outdone. 'And Karl Marx lived around the corner.'

Bloomsbury seems a curiously classless area, a place that hasn't really changed since I first visited it almost twenty-five years ago. I caught sight of a client of mine feeding a stray cat through the railings of the gardens but we proceeded on to **Grafton Way** and across **Tottenham Court Road** to **Gower Street**. This is a good sniffing street if you're a dog interested in tree trunks but hopelessly boring if you're walking the dog. The gardens of University College looked foreboding to dog-walkers so we hiked around the college via **Gower Place** to **Gordon Street**, but first I told Julia a story. Jeremy Bentham, the eighteenth-century moralist, the man who said that the question is not whether animals feel pain but rather whether they suffer, Bentham, the first humanist to articulate the proposition that animals have inherent rights, who died in 1832, still attends senate meetings at University College. His mummy is brought out for the occasions.

Julia didn't believe me, so I went no further and we continued on and into **Gordon Square**. Dogs aren't allowed in Gordon Square but as the signs were missing and I knew that the gardener likes dogs we entered. 'Virginia Woolf used to stroll here with Lytton Strachey and John Maynard Keynes,' Julia explained.

I took her to the middle of the gardens to show her a massively flamboyant weeping ash and a bird's nest-like weeping elm, but she was much more preoccupied with a weeping man. I reined the dogs in and we passed by with silence and respect, heading for the southern exit. I felt a resistance in Julia's arm and knew that instinctively she wanted to just quietly sit down beside him, help dab his eyes but say nothing – just be there. She squeezed my arm. 'It wouldn't really matter if he were some young trendy long-haired man in jeans, but there's nothing more sorrowful than seeing someone like that, a mature, pinstripe-suited man crying. I feel awful.' So did I.

We turned left out of Gordon Square and immediately into **Tavistock Square**. The Camden Council sign stated that dogs must be kept on leads, but I saw others that were not, so Lib and Lex were given their freedom and ran off in separate directions. 'Virginia Woolf lived here too,' Julia murmured.

It's always a moral dilemma as to whether to leash or unleash dogs in circumstances such as these. The letter of the law is obviously clear but then again, so is its lack of implementation. The gardeners were paying no attention at all to the freely roaming canines. The result is that in these circumstances I become an active follower, not a leader, and blend in my activities with those of the locals. The dogs were grateful.

Liberty investigated the undercarriage of a black and tan mongrel that was peeing on Councillor Mrs Miller's Hiroshima memorial plaque while Lex went off to contemplate a rather sophisticated young cocker spaniel being walked by both its owners, a couple in their early thirties. The spaniel was digging under the copper beech tree that Pandit Nehru planted when the Gandhi statue in the centre of the gardens was unveiled.

'Looking for something?' I asked his owners.

'Oh no. He's simply being destructive. This is why we bring him to work with us each day. If we leave him at home he does the same to our carpets.'

He had an innocent face like Lexington's, which is perhaps why she was interested in him. Liberty in the meantime had been less successful. The black and tan, together with his German shepherd-type cohort and their owner, were all leaving the southern exit, closely watched by a lady with a large shopping bag.

When these dogs had departed and we had moved away, our observer started feeding the feral pigeons. They flocked from all corners of the gardens to her, as did the crows that patrolled on the periphery. She finished her work and walked down in our direction where there is a fenced-off area in the gardens.

'Excuse me,' asked Julia. 'Do you know why this part of the gardens is fenced off?'

'No disrespect to your dogs, I love dogs, but they can carry diseases and this area is for children. I used to have a dog but I just had to have her put down. Smothered in cancer. It was the kindest thing. I took her to the hospital and they told me that nothing could be done. The dog's your best friend, you know, when you're on your own and all. I love animals. Now that I don't have my dog I come here each day and bring bread for the pigeons and chops for the carrion crows. Are those Blue Peter dogs?'

We humans certainly are a gregarious species. We crave companionship and suffer when we lack it. The scientific evidence is quite clear. The chance of developing a serious illness such as heart disease or cancer increases dramatically when relationships are broken but, curiously, the lethal effect of broken relationships, of deaths or divorces, is eliminated if another relationship is rapidly formed. Perhaps that's why individuals like this lady, people who live alone, are so likely to have pet dogs or cats in the first place and perhaps that's why, almost instinctively, she has replaced her lost dog with the Tavistock Square pigeons and crows.

Leads were restored to their respective dogs and we walked them down **Bedford Way**, past a group of lanky young Scandinavians coming out of their hotel, all of whom had both the same hair colour and style as my retrievers, and approached **Russell Square**. This entire area was once the speculative venture of a carpenter, Thomas Cubitt, now the patron saint of estate agents. It's a large and noisy square with rose beds, garish fountains and many signs reminding owners that their dogs must be kept on leads. Canine skid marks in the mud under the massive plane trees suggested that here too the regulation is breached and the dogs are let free.

I was starving, so I headed for the restaurant kiosk and had a bacon sandwich that wasn't fit for a dog. I threw it out. Smartly dressed young ladies with Samsonite briefcases sat at the outdoor restaurant tables eating late breakfasts of eggs, beans, chips and ketchup while bag ladies shuffled past and shoeless drunks stretched out on the grass. A black American cocker spaniel raced round the statue of the Duke of Bedford, barking incessantly, oblivious to the large white mutt and its small German shepherd-type companion who were on a scavenging expedition with their elderly lady owner. A Lhasa Apso (or was it a Shih Tzu?) danced past on the end of his lead, its tail contorted into happy position number one, curled in a circle over its back, and a Rottweiler was being marched briskly from the south-west to north-east corners of the gardens by his punk-style owners without being given the opportunity to sniff a blade of grass, let alone a dog's ear. Liberty and Lexington in the meantime had found a harem of two West Highland terriers and a Yorkshire terrier.

As they approached, the Yorkie barked out a warning and her owner apologised. 'Please don't pay any attention to old bossy boots. She barks at anything that moves and most things that don't as well.'

Liberty was undeterred by the noise and stood expectantly over the terrier. Lex watched from a distance.

'She belonged to two old ladies near Clapham Common but they got beat up and 'ad to move into a home. Couldn't take the dog. Now 'e's me 'usband's dog. Wouldn't part with 'er for the world.'

The Westies were hers, mother and daughter. 'I sat up all night when she 'ad 'er pups. I was so chuffed. She did it all 'erself. I was more excited than when I 'ad me own baby. I was all choked up.'

The dogs meantime had formed a racing circuit with the younger Westie as the leader and were churning up mud as they raced in a figure of eight around the park side of the duke's statue.

'How could you part with the litter?' I asked and was told that she couldn't. Friends have the other pups and she sees them regularly.

'Take care if you're coming back 'ere with your dogs,' she advised as we departed. 'There are two Rottweilers that are brought 'ere each day that 'ave no discipline.'

**Bedford Place**, a bed-and-breakfast-lined street, led us on to **Bloomsbury Square** with the British Museum to the right. Once this must have been an exciting place to live. Samuel Butler recounted walking from Bloomsbury Square past the British Museum – one morning in May 1883, to be exact – and seeing the entire steps and courtyard of the museum covered in stuffed birds on their way to their new home at the Natural History Museum in South Kensington. He found it 'very pretty and very droll'. Blooms-bury Square today is nondescript. Young men sat about feeding McDonalds hamburgers to pigeons. The dogs raced about and found nothing of interest. Winos littered the benches. The sign at the entrance stated that 'No person shall suffer any dog to remain in the pleasure garden.' So, as it was neither a pleasure for them nor for us, leads were reapplied and we crossed the road and walked through the arcade of shops on **Sicilian Avenue**, across **Kingsway** and then left through one of the alleys leading into **Lincoln's Inn Fields**.

'Is it lined with maple trees?' Julia queried, seeing the sign, 'Canada Walk', but it was not, rather their boring cousin the London plane. Dogs are allowed on the periphery of the park but not in the enclosures at the west end, which I explained to my dogs as I took off their leads.

A man with a face as stern as Buster Keaton's walked along with his Jack Russell sharing his chocolate bar with it, a square for himself, a square for the dog, while at the Lincoln's Inn end a chauffeur stood to attention beside a turquoise Rolls-Royce as his mistress walked her shuffling Peke and a reluctant pup. Men in suits with deeply cut side vents marched past taking long measured strides followed by younger women, all in black, carrying sheafs of documents.

'This is where I came to learn what to wear when I played the barrister in that series I did with Peter Barkworth, *Late Starter*,' Julia commented. 'I sat in Lincoln's Inn for two days just watching what they wore and how they carried themselves.'

I remembered that series well. For the year the chief worked on it I lived with a prosecuting attorney. 'Why didn't you eat your Brussels sprouts? Exactly when did you develop an aversion to my Brussels sprouts? If you eat my mother's Brussels sprouts, why haven't you eaten these Brussels sprouts?' We married when she was playing Lulu, a sex kitten. Taking that role home from work was at least more sustaining.

Other actresses have long had associations with Lincoln's Inn Fields. Nell Gwynne's lover Charles Sackville lived here and if you venture into the basement of the extraordinary Sir John Soane's Museum at number 13 and look out of the window you will see a massively grotesque tomb on which is inscribed, 'Alas, Poor Fanny'. Fanny was Sarah Siddons' favourite dog.

Our favourite dogs, in the meantime, had found Sally the beagle, the second Sally of the morning, and a black and white terrier pup. 'Sally was slowin' down, loike, so I got 'er the pup when 'e was ten weeks old to loiven 'er up, loike. Cert'nly 'as.'

Lincoln's Inn itself is only open to the public from noon until 2.30 p.m. and only dogs of residents are permitted inside, so we continued walking back down the middle of the fields to watch a netball game being played by grown-up women dressed in school-girl sports kit. Two games were in fact being played on both sides of the central cupola, with all four teams in different coloured but matching uniforms of short pleated skirts and cotton blouses on the backs of which were letters indicating floor positions. Around the periphery of the games were pinstripe-suited businessmen observers, some of whom were down on their hands and knees as they offered encouragement to the lady players. The City netball league was in action and I was flummoxed.

'How do you find the time?' I asked one of the substitute players standing at the edge.

'We're given time off work.'

'Who do you work for?'

'BP.'

Amazing. Staff are given time off to play games for other staff to ogle at in the heart of the day and in the heart of London. I wanted to stay and watch, but the commander locked her arm on to mine and we marched on. The dogs weren't interested in staying either.

We passed the Royal College of Surgeons on the left with the fields' tennis courts on our right. Bat boxes are nailed to all of the massive plane trees in the fields but none were visible at this end. Julia was enchanted by another weeping elm tree, similar in age to the one in Gordon Square, and she stood under it for a time marvelling at the intricacy of the branch formation.

The dogs were more interested in a tiny Maltese terrier, no more than eight weeks old, a snow white cotton fluff of a pup. I didn't want my dogs to frighten it and walked over to its owner, a weather-beaten man in a comfortable-looking jumper, ageing tweed jacket and slippers.

'I know what you're going to tell me, but my vet has told me it's quite safe to let the pup down now before his jabs are completed.'

That's *my* line to pet owners and I surveyed both owner and pup trying to recognise them but I couldn't.

'I was just coming over to make sure my dogs didn't bother yours,' I said, 'but I agree with your vet. I'm a vet and I think it's safe too, and besides, this is the time in their lives when their personalities are set for life. It's good for pups to be exposed to as much of what they will meet later in life now while they're still young. It makes them more reliable later on.'

He didn't recognise me either. It was a safe encounter.

'You a vet eh? Well, you might be interested in my wife's old dog. Her old Maltese died just a few weeks ago when she was twenty-one years old and this gave us a problem. My wife wants to be buried with the dog and I didn't know what to do with the dog's remains. I thought of our freezer, but that didn't seem quite right, so I contacted the Natural History Museum and found a taxidermist. Easier than getting a plumber. I had to catch a bus, just over there on Aldwych, but by then the old bugger had been dead for a few days and as I stood in the queue the lady beside me said, "What've we got in the bag, then? A dead body?" "Got it in one, luv," I replied. The taxidermist's done a marvellous job and the old dog's back with us now, waiting for my wife.'

Julia missed it all. She was preventing Liberty and Lex from eating rust-coloured mushrooms growing near the western exit –

no doubt a mycological reminder of some ancient pet that got buried, not stuffed.

With leads back on, we walked past a French car with German licence plates in which there was a hunt terrier balancing upon a pair of green hunter boots. Julia pointed out The Old Curiosity Shop down Portugal Street, which I had never seen before, and we walked back and across Kingsway on to **Wild Street** and through the **Peabody Estate**.

The Peabody Charitable Trust is perhaps the last truly Victorian landlord in London and the Covent Garden Estate on Wild Street is typical of their blocks of flats. The charity maintains its paternalistic attitude towards its tenants and stipulates that dogs are not permitted on their estates. This was undoubtedly a wise precaution when the estates were built in the 1800s, as dogs and cats had always heavily populated this area. Samuel Pepys estimated that 40,000 dogs and 200,000 cats were killed within days during the Great Plague when the Lord Mayor ordered their deaths on the unfortunate assumption that they caused the disease (which in fact only made it easier for rats to survive and rat fleas to spread it). This was always a rough and rowdy area, 'with bricks and dead cats thrown at the candidates of local elections', according to one writer.

The Peabody dictat is antiquated today. Those who can benefit most from the companionship of a pet are the old dears who now inhabit this estate and I see several who smuggle their pets in and out in shopping baskets for their exercise in Lincoln's Inn Fields so that their landlords won't know.

The dogs diligently marched through the estate looking neither left nor right, past a querulous-looking cat sitting in a window, then along **Kemble Street** to **Drury Lane**. Nell Gwynne lived here, which made it pretty easy for her to nip over to see Charles Sackville in Lincoln's Inn Fields. Drury Lane is the dirty back door of the new sanitised Covent Garden and it contains the only remaining speck of 'garden' in the area, **Drury Lane Gardens**, a postage stamp of raised green where a posted sign stipulates that 'A person in a verminous or offensively filthy condition shall not lie upon or occupy any seat in this open space'. That said enough about the place for us, so we missed it and walked on, turning left through the old **Bartlett Court** housing estate past a young woman in torn black tights, short skirt and leather jacket peeing by the wall.

'Sordid,' I thought.

'No liketee,' said Julia.

The dogs sniffed, but the pheromones were human not canine, so with high heads they floated on and up to the trees of **Broad Court**, the trunks of which smelled infinitely more enjoyable.

Broad Court enters **Bow Street** at its junction with **Long Acre** and Julia now needed blinkers to walk down Long Acre, her 'best' Covent Garden street. Her favourite arts supply shop is here, on both sides of the road, but she survived and we reached **St Martin's Lane**. Upon crossing the road, I commanded my dogs to sit and stare in silence for two minutes at the Renault showroom. Although there is nothing to indicate the great canine happening that occurred here, it was at a coffee house on this site that a group of men gathered in 1824 and formed the first animal protection society anywhere in the world, later to become the Royal Society for the Prevention of Cruelty to Animals.

On we marched into **Leicester Square**. There was not a dog in sight, nor any other mammal other than humans. The gardens were filled with winos and bag ladies. A couple of spaced-out teenagers lurched along the path on the eastern side, both looking a deathly grey. Most of the starlings had already vacated to the suburbs for the day, though they would be back in the evening. I let the dogs off their leads and they scampered in the fallen leaves when suddenly all the sparrows and pigeons in the trees took flight. Liberty jumped as if given a swift kick and ran off to the far corner. I was surprised that my dogs could have such an effect, but then Julia pointed up to the sky where a kestrel was cruising overhead. Kestrels can't find their favourite field mice and voles in London, so they eat other birds, especially sparrows, and perhaps unwary young golden retrievers too. The autumn congregations of starlings here are absolutely astounding. You need an umbrella if you walk through the square at nightfall. This isn't a new phenomenon, however. Almost thirty years ago, Big Ben failed to chime at nine one evening because of the weight of starlings on the hour hand.

As we called back our dogs, dwarfs started singing all around us. 'Heigh-ho, heigh-ho, it's off to work we go...' The sound was coming from the Odeon cinema where *Snow White* was about to open. Suddenly there were smiles on every face: bag ladies, winos, druggies, Japanese tourists, Chinese waiters, office workers, UB40s and two dog-walkers. Two men in a cradle high up the side of a building danced to the tune. The sound memory of the tune seemingly imprinted into all our brains evoked a reminiscence of contentment throughout the whole human mass in this rather seedy square.

Leicester Square has always had a magnetic attraction for some of the flakier members of society. In 1724, a surgeon at Westminster Hospital, one Nathaniel St André, claimed that a woman had given birth to fifteen bunny rabbits here after being frightened by a big bunny rabbit. He had personally delivered two of them. King George I was intrigued and sent over his court surgeon, who delivered another one. This, of course, became a minor sensation and the woman turned into a local celebrity. Her fame was fleeting, however, as shortly after these births she was seen buying some more very small bunny rabbits at the local market, which just goes to prove that there's nothing new under the sun.

The rain was still holding off as we left Leicester Square and walked up **Wardour Street** to the churchyard of **St Anne's, Soho**, now a Westminster public park, complete with the requisite dog-dirt bins. We walked up the stairs to the raised green space, raised because we were walking on at least 10,000 bodies. My curiosity overwhelmed me and I inspected the canine-emissions containers. They were filled with Kentucky Fried Chicken boxes and, yes, ample gift-wrapped dog dirt. From my immediate analysis only very large dogs were discharging their faeces into these receptacles, but then again they were quite high bins.

Liberty and Lexington, once more off their leads, danced about while two black cats maintained an eyeball-to-eyeball motionless confrontation in the far nothern corner of the yard. One soon left, in a nonchalant insouciant way, while at the same moment a German shepherd ventured up the steps, looked about the area, then immediately turned around and left. Lib was about to follow when I shouted to her to stop. She did.

This patch of greenery is where actresses who can't be parted from their dogs, either because they love them too much or don't have anyone at home to look after them, come for canine exercise between performances on matinée days. Show dogs used to come here too, but there aren't any on Shaftesbury Avenue right now, only two Burmese cats, Fortnum and his understudy Mason. We sat down in front of a row of tombstones and watched the dogs rummage in the grass. Little did they know that they were rummaging through the ashes of the creator of Lord Peter Wimsey, Dorothy L. Sayers, scattered here after her funeral in 1957.

A stout lady carrying a Budgen bag forced herself up the stairs, and waddled over to where the remaining black cat was lying. The cat knew her, for it greeted her as she approached. From the bag the lady withdrew a McDonalds hamburger container and filled it with cat food from an already opened can. Two crows watched intently but my dogs paid no heed. They were much more interested in two scar-faced Dobermanns ushered in by their buxom mistress, all of whom I recognised from my practice. She was a lady of the twilight on neighbouring Berwick Street and the dogs were her professional minders, the only problem being that they fought with each other over *her* rather than simply handling the more offensive punters. I'm constantly patching up those two dogs.

We roped in our companions before any unpleasant incident occurred, exchanged smiles and greetings and left through **Berwick Street** market: fruit, vegetables, stone-washed jeans, tape cassettes, shirts and scarves, all being loudly hawked by the Cockney stall-holders. This is my wife's spiritual home. Stall-keepers shouted their 'Hi Julie's and she beamed with pleasure. All I could think of was cheese and what a clever man Samuel Pepys was to bury his Parmesan cheeses first before fleeing the Great Fire of London.

I suggested that we nip into the St James's Tavern for a quick ploughman's and a drink but the weather worried the boss so we marched on. Virtually all of these pubs have dogs and I know them simply because mine is the nearest veterinary practice. What I didn't know, until it was explained to me by one of the local publicans, is that dog and rat contests were common in these pubs in Victorian times. It was the poor man's sport. Many of the pubs had rat pits in a back room into which small terrier dogs were dropped. The dog that killed the most rats was the winner, although of course many dogs must themselves have died from multiple rat bites. The police turned a blind eye on both the gambling and the savagery of the encounters quite simply because it was an effective method of rat control.

**Rupert Street**, the continuation of Berwick Street, took us down to **Shaftesbury Avenue** and then to **Piccadilly Circus**. We crossed Piccadilly Circus and turned on to **Jermyn Street**, with its elegant shops and 'Peg's Fancies' and 'Brown Cows' at Fortnum & Mason's soda fountain, another of the highlights in Julia's life. This was a dog walk, however, not a window shop, so I forced her left on to **Duke of York Street** and down to **St James's Square**. We walked in single file with Lexington leading and crossed into the square.

Signs on the entrances to the gardens quite specifically state 'No Dogs Allowed', but the fastest way to the other side was straight through the middle and as the first drops of rain were starting to fall we took this course, only meeting two other people in the gardens, both with dogs. The first was a cairn with a cairn-type owner – short, stocky, a little ill-kempt and unshaven that day. The other was a black and white sheepdog with his young female owner. The gardens themselves are exquisite, with ornamental cherry, blackthorn and mulberry around the periphery and magnificent mature trees throughout. St James's Square is a real garden, unlike any that we had walked through that morning. Julia stopped at the fig tree at the southern end and scoured it for signs of ripe figs. There were thousands of fat but unripe green ones, but I have never found a way of bringing these on if they are picked green; in fact, the only time I have known figs to ripen outdoors in London was after the warm summer of 1976. I walked on with Lexington on her lead and met a pretty young woman who smiled at me. The chief noticed and said that people who smile at you when you're out walking your dog are infinitely more attractive than those who don't, a fairly safe judgement which I knew was based upon the smile she had just received on Duke of York Street from a Leonard Bernstein lookalike.

Rain was now coming down more heavily as we crossed **Pall Mall** and walked up **Carlton Gardens** where we turned left on to **Carlton House Terrace** to reach the steps down to **The Mall**. The building just before the steps was at one time the German Embassy and there, beneath a massive plane tree, surrounded by statues to past British military heroes, rests the only official marker of the Nazi presence in London, the tombstone of Giro, the Nazi Ambassador Leopold van Hoesch's dog. It reads, in German, 'To Giro, a true friend'. An inconsequential memento of an evil presence perhaps as well as any other exemplifying Hannah Arendt's thesis on the banality of evil.

We scampered down the steps, past a very fluffy golden retriever and into **St James's Park**, the end of this leg of the walk. Today was going to be a 'dry' walk – no dog swims – but Lexington had cheated earlier in the morning. The walk had been more exciting for us than the dogs, for once, and now they deserved a treat. With rain pelting down we walked with them to the lake where they frolicked with delight. Real water dogs. It refreshed them, but with the inclement weather we humans had had enough for the day.

57

# Walk Four

## St James's Park to Hyde Park

START: The Mall and Horse
Guards Road intersection of
St James's Park, SW1.

END: Brook Gate (Marble Arch)
entrance to Hyde Park, W1.

LENGTH: Approximately 3 miles.

TIME: Approximately 2 hours.

LEADS: Required in Berkeley
Square.

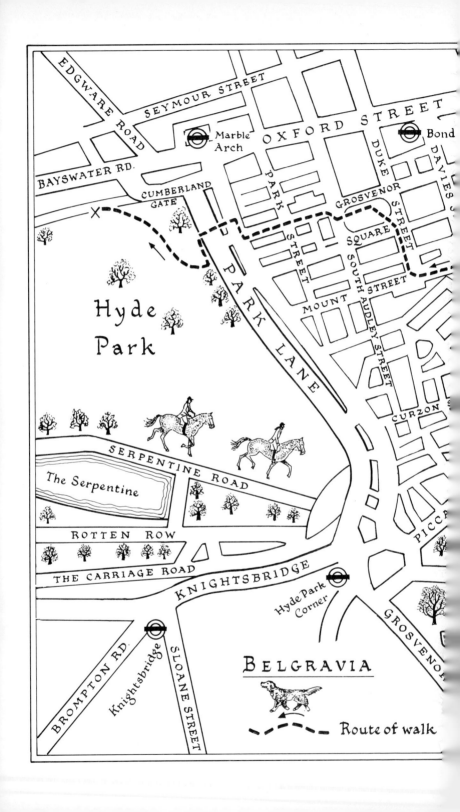

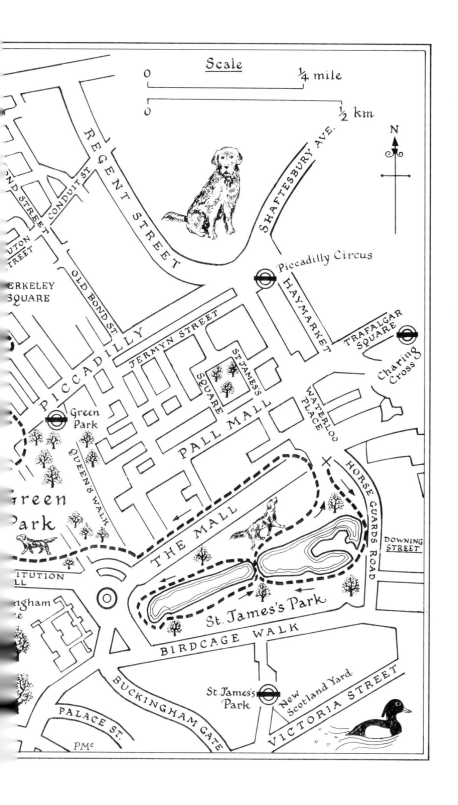

# Walk Four...

## The second 'dog leg', from St James's park via Mayfair to Hyde Park

It was as if some omnipotent vandal had desecrated the Garden of Eden. Only days before we had been here, by Duck Island in St James's Park, and had wallowed in the gentle, dignified and serene beauty of this most elegant of London's green space. But in the interval a gale of hurricane force winds ravaged the city. Weeping willows lay drowning in the lake. Plane trees were dismembered or fully uprooted, their entrails lying in a tangle of grass and earth against the eerie peacefulness of a too-blue sky. The scene was surreal and uncompromising in its power.

The four lines of trees along The Mall, leading to Buckingham Palace survived, giving a deceptive air of normality to drivers going past, but as we walked around the Whitehall end of the lake the enormity and irreversibility of the destruction became too apparent. Liberty and Lexington, of course, thought that this was the most heaven-sent of gifts. Liberty found a dead pigeon and in a state of near revery rolled on it. Lexington raced back and forth carrying a fallen branch, drooling at the multitudes of ducks and geese on the lake and on Duck Island.

St James's park is primarily the work of King Charles II. He laid out The Mall for playing pall mall, although the court itself, similar to the one we saw at The Freemasons Arms in Hampstead, disappeared centuries ago. The Mall used to come to a dead end at the old village of Charing, where Admiralty Arch now stands. The lake was originally laid out as a canal and St James's Park was to be Britain's answer to Versailles. Samuel Pepys wrote of coming here after the Great Fire to 'lay down upon the grass by the canal and sleep awhile', and no doubt dream of his buried Parmesan cheeses. Capability Brown remodelled the park in the eighteenth century, but it was John Nash, the force behind the creation of Regent's Park, who in 1829 introduced the curvaceous and informal look that the hurricane of 1987 has now so deeply wounded. Fish, weeds and plankton thrive in St James's lake because of the freshness of the artesian water and this is one reason why there is such a variety of waterfowl.

'Liberty! Come here this instant! If you so much as look at that duck once more you are going home!'

The boss was in no mood for canine shenanigans as she bellowed her conditional clauses at her dogs. The strange fact is that, having just been let off the leads at the corner of the park, they seemed to understand these subjunctives and obediently ran off at a tangent, away from the lake, towards a fallen plane tree where they engaged in a jaw wrestle over a branch. So far nary the sight of another dog. In fact, few natives were visible. Most park visitors were in standard tourist garb. Middle-aged American couples in matching designer track shoes and wearing raincoats that fold up into nothing when packed in suitcases strolled past taking wide-angle pictures of the ducks and geese with fixed focus 35mm cameras. Small groups of Japanese tourists, all with pocket guides to London in their hands, all immaculately turned out – the women in Burberry tartan skirts and hats and the men in sober dark suits – took photos of themselves and of each other, with Nikons and Canons which probably make four-minute eggs as well.

'Wonderful dogs,' an angular and healthy-looking man commented as we passed on the Birdcage Walk side of the lake. 'They are so intelligent. We use them in Switzerland as dogs for the blind.'

I agreed with him. Retrievers are bred to serve and make ideal 'service dogs'. Lexington could be trained with great ease to work to the gun, engage in field trials or serve as a guide dog for the blind. She has the right willingness of spirit, ability to learn and desire to please, a desire that, in absolute canine terms, is actually an inherent subservience to 'masters'; she has the three qualities that are necessary for any successful training. Liberty, on the other hand, is a loser. I know of a guide dog that one day, after some minor surgery, walked his master to a traffic island in the middle of a busy dual carriageway, then sat down and refused to budge. He was probably one of Lib's relatives.

A human traffic jam was forming ahead at the bridge over the lake as a Canada goose escorted her surprisingly young goslings across the path and into the water. It was, after all, exactly mid-October. As we waited with Lib and Lex at heel we saw in the distance by Birdcage Walk a Cavalier King Charles spaniel being marched along at double time. This is almost but not quite what I had wanted to see, for King Charles II was the designer of the original King Charles spaniel and St James's is where he used to walk his dogs. These dogs have squashed faces like pugs. They are true brachycephalics. Cavalier King Charles spaniels are twentieth-century creations, bred from the original model, but with noses

63

that work. In London they have become one of the most popular small dogs, not for their intelligence – which even their owners will acknowledge is vestigial – but for their gentle benevolence. I have never, and I mean *never*, met a vicious Cavalier King Charles spaniel. It is often said that dogs come to look like their owners, but this isn't exactly true. People choose dogs that they feel comfortable with, which means that the dogs often share personality traits with their owners. Ronald and Nancy Reagan tried a schnauzer but Nancy ended up getting dragged around like a balloon on the end of a lead. They acknowledged their mistake and chose a Cavalier as the replacement. Not too bright but 'rilly nice', a perfect mirror of its masters.

As we walked across the bridge, the feathered multitudes became almost overwhelming. James I kept cassowaries and cormorants here, but it was Charles II who laid out long rows of aviaries for his entertainment – Birdcage Walk – and added exotic geese and ducks. He also introduced duck decoys on the lake and pinioned his birds so that they would not fly off, in the process establishing the lake for what it is today, a major transit stop for wild birds.

Pelicans were introduced also by Charles II, when a pair was presented to him as a gift from the Russian Ambassador. One of these pendulous-looking pouch-bills recently found a new delicacy, feral pigeon. He'd capture one, hold it underwater to drown it and eat it whole. On its own this wasn't much of a problem, until he developed a taste for duckling! Which is when the park gamekeepers became concerned. When, at a sitting, he polished off a full brood of snow goose goslings, he was whipped off to gaol in perpetuity at Regent's Park Zoo. A friend with a similar inclination went with him.

We continued across the bridge. Lex looked wistfully at all the feathers – mallards, Canada geese, myriads of coots and dabchicks, even a Carolina wood duck, when Julia suddenly stopped and squeezed my arm. 'Look! It's horrid! I hate it!'

I looked, but I didn't see.

'The pigeons. They're horrid.'

On a tree at the end of a bridge, a tree that had been denuded by the storm, perched over fifty ruffled and dishevelled-looking feral pigeons. Feral pigeons don't normally perch on trees as wood pigeons do. They are the urban descendants of rock doves, cliff dwellers, and treat the buildings of London as their cliffs. True feral pigeons have two prominent black wing bars, white rumps and glossy green necks. Birds with other colourings have been diluted with domestic or racing-pigeon blood. These silent hunch-backs were all the colour of the wild rock dove, true ferals, and they broodily observed us as we walked on.

Julia moved to the far side of the bridge, past a male 'Jack spaniel' dog leering at the flesh in the water below, and suddenly burbled with joy. 'I don't believe it. Look. It's amazing.'

I looked. There were gulls, black and white tufted ducks, mallards and Canada geese in the water. On the shore were sparrows and a robin. The swamp cypresses were proudly erect, seemingly untouched by the hurricane.

'Over there. In the corner.'

I saw nothing.

'Parsley. There's garden parsley.'

So there was and, with aplomb and a hint of chauvinism, I leapt the fence and went under the bridge where I picked a sprig from its crack in the concrete. Garden parsley growing wild under the bridge by the water's edge in St James's park would have been an exciting find had I not already known that the peripatetic Rosalind Hadden, tabulator of all wild plants in the West End, had found some garden parsley sprouting from a wall on Montagu Street, around the corner from my veterinary clinic, or that she had seen knotted hedge parsley growing from the wall of St Mary's Church, right across York Street from my practice.

Having crossed the bridge, we continued on The Mall side of the park towards Buckingham Palace. Only two dogs seen so far and mine were beginning to suffer withdrawal symptoms. Liberty spied a grey squirrel in a bed of universal pansies and in a flash succumbed to an avalanche of primitive bloodlust. Her hackles went up, her ears leapt forward, her tail stood as erect as a golden retriever's can and she charged the rodent. At the sight of Liberty's behaviour, Lexington's pack instinct overwhelmed her and, parroting her leader's actions, she too leapt at full speed at the defenceless creature. Julia cried out commands but without success. Charging from two angles, the dogs cornered the squirrel between two plane trees but, at the last instant, it leapt like a kangaroo mouse above their jaws and on to a tree. The dogs stood excitedly hound-like beneath the tree – until Julia got to them a second later.

'Don't you *ever* do that again,' she screamed at Liberty as she smacked her face.

Liberty cowered and, at the sight of Julia coming towards her,

Lexington rolled over as a supplicant before an all-powerful deity. Tourists were befuddled as Julia disciplined the dogs. They had not seen our pets' precipitating behaviour. I took notes.

I have mixed feelings about grey squirrels. On the one hand, they are vividly active creatures, robust solid mammals that I am happy to tend when injured ones are brought in for repairs. Squirrels aren't too good at judging distances when branches are gusting and they concuss themselves sufficiently to allow people to pick them up, box them and bring them to me for treatment. More frequently, they get caught by marauding terriers and I'm presented with twitching 500-gram masses of solid muscle and fur, in deep shock and unlikely to recover.

I feel a mild kinship with these creatures because, like me, they are fairly recent North American transplants to London. The first grey squirrels were released by some Americans in Bushy Park, Middlesex, and Kingston Hill, Surrey, at the end of the last century. Early this century, the Duke of Bedford, the descendant of the duke whose statue is in Russell Square, released squirrels into Regent's Park, and it was only a short time before they oozed over London to become the dog's delight and the gardener's nightmare. In 1923 squirrels were seen swimming the Thames and subsequently spread throughout South London, although it wasn't until the thirties that they crossed the Lea into east London. By that time their numbers had increased to such an extent that thousands were shot throughout London in an attempt to slow their progression. Even a major distemper outbreak amongst them in the 1940s only temporarily slowed their onslaught.

The problem is that, although they are 'cute', they are amazingly destructive. In the winter they will eat the bark off trees, sometimes 'ringing' the tree in a way that unwittingly prevents food and nourishment getting up the tree trunk. In spring they nip off and consume the succulent sap-filled buds of trees and shrubs, seriously interfering with natural growth. Later on they raid birds' nests and eat the eggs of hatchlings. That's why park keepers are not at all concerned when dogs act as mine did. Park visitors, myself included, on the other hand, revel in squirrel antics. As far as Julia is concerned her dogs should simply be above such primitive and uncontrolled behaviour. They might not be people but they certainly aren't as animal as other animals and there is no place for carnivorous behaviour in their activities.

The dogs were marched to heel back to the path, then on along the lake side. A few minutes later they were once more given their freedom whereupon they trotted to the top of the lake and went in. Swans came to investigate my large golden carp and Julia commanded both of the dogs to leave the lake, which they did. We continued around the top of the water where the dogs entered it once more. This time they were met by four white swans and one black one.

'Is that white line on the black swan's red beak its mark?' Julia asked.

I couldn't answer. The black swan is an Australian native but the indigenous white swan has been marked, plentiful and almost tame, for hundreds of years. Today more die from eating lead shot or lead weights than from any other cause, and most veterinarians who work close to the Thames have become accustomed to treating these noble animals for lead-poisoning.

In times past we humans were more obviously their biggest enemies. The Venetian Ambassador, as long ago as 1492, when Christopher Columbus was on his first visit to America, wrote to the Venetian Doge that, 'It is a truly beautiful thing to behold one or two thousand tame swans upon the river Thames.' Tame they might have been, but so too were they a staple part of the gastronome's diet. At one Inner Temple feast alone, in 1532, 168 swans were eaten. Now they were about to seek their revenge upon my rather innocent young pets and once more we commanded the dogs to leave the water to the waterproofed and return to land.

Continuing our figure of eight around the lake we met dog number three, an Irish water spaniel being walked by a Sloane-type lady in Barbour jacket and green wellies. I had seen many countrified walkers this morning, but this woman was the first with a dog.

'Is that an Irish water spaniel?' I asked innocently.

'Had to trim her. She was going all Rastafarian and lumpy.' And smelly I bet.

The impact of the recent storm was overwhelming once more as we headed back towards Whitehall. Full and mature trees that had been seemingly immune to any insult, lay uprooted and fallen as if they were straws in sand.

A man of about sixty years of age in cavalry twill trousers and with a military bearing was standing beside a doddery old Staffordshire bull terrier that was sniffing the gate at the entrance to the children's play area.

'Oh, I do like old dogs,' Julia sighed to me as we passed.

'You wouldn't like this one,' the bull terrier's owner countered. 'She smells so badly that my wife has asked me for a new three-piece suite. I've told her we should simply burn the chair that the dog sleeps on, preferably with the dog still on it!'

I wasn't going to get involved in veterinary advice, but his comment raised the question of exactly how much damage pets cause each year. There are over thirteen million dogs and cats in Britain and if you assume that each one causes some damage each year – torn curtains, soiled carpets, personal injuries, absence from work – and if you arbitrarily assume that the yearly loss is eighty pounds per pet, that means that pets cause over a billion pounds' worth of damage yearly – a mere blip in Stock Market terms but nevertheless a potent engine of the economy!

As we completed our figure of eight and neared the bridge across the lake once more, Lexington started digging furiously in the leaves beneath a fallen plane tree and proudly paraded her treasure for us, a garden snail. I removed it from her mouth, threw it away and we crossed the bridge again, proceeding along the far side towards Whitehall still. So far it had been a remarkably dogless morning and in consequence we had met few people. In the distance I spied the Jack spaniel seen previously on the bridge, this time making an absolute nuisance of himself as he tried to prepare his own duck *à l'orange*. His elderly owner in vain tried to catch him as he torpedoed through the aviary of wildfowl.

'He really is the apple of his mistress's eye,' confided his owner's friend to us as we passed. 'He can do no wrong, but he has no discipline.'

We rather pompously instructed our canines to walk to heel and walked on, not mentioning the squirrel incident, and, having completed the circuit, crossed The Mall to turn and walk back along its north side towards **Buckingham Palace** and **Green Park**.

'Not very doggy,' Julia commented. 'Not even a corgi in sight.'

Nor would there be. The Queen's corgis have been a bit in the doghouse recently and have needed some stern treatment. It seems that they started to act like a pack and when they accidentally injured the Queen Mother, a man with an understanding of canine behaviour was called in to advise. It only took him a short time to realise that one of the dogs, a seven-year-old bitch, had taken over as pack leader and was leading the others in their errant ways. The Queen was advised that this dog should be separated from the others and housed where it would receive sensible and stern discipline. It took the Queen only seconds to resolve this problem and it was arranged that the troublemaker be immediately rehomed – with Princess Anne! Since then there have been virtually no further problems from the remaining corgis and *none* whatsoever from the delinquent.

The leaves along the grassy embankment in front of **Carlton House** and **Marlborough House** were knee-deep from the storm and bone dry. Liberty had a leaf fit and tore about tunnelling, leaping, diving and turning on a sixpence. Twice she ran over Lexington. Lex tried to join in, but as she did so I commanded Lib to stop, for she was endangering passers-by. Two elderly Cavalier King Charles spaniels being walked on the grass by a chauffeur paused and peered at Liberty but did little else. My dogs showed no interest in them. The leaves were more lively than these mummified canines.

We passed **St James's Palace** and continued along the front of **Lancaster House**, past **Milkmaid's Passage**, which leads up towards Piccadilly alongside Lancaster House and is so called because for almost two centuries St James's Park was the main London venue for licensed milk-sellers with their cows. As late as 1905, cows still appeared daily to supply milk directly to the customer. Today, instead of cows, there were three mounted video cameras monitoring my dogs' behaviour as they entered **Green Park**.

Green Park is relatively lifeless compared to other royal parks – no water, no flower beds, and only one statue. It seems to exist simply as an afterthought, a green access from St James's Park to Hyde Park. It was not always so. This was once Upper St James's Park, the most fashionable venue in which to be seen. The glitterati of the eighteenth century appeared here in outrageous dress and committed acts that would today get their names into the gossip pages of the tabloids and also have the RSPCA breathing down their necks. Balloon ascents were fashionable, and relatively safe because of the sparcity of trees. One man made his balloon ascent astride his horse while a Mrs Graham, upon ascending above the park in her balloon, dropped live monkeys in parachutes to her friends below.

Charles II added an ice house and snow house to the park, the contours of which can still be seen today as hillocks near the centre, so that he could indulge in iced drinks in the summer as his French alter ego did.

With Buckingham Palace to the left, King George IV's London *pied à terre* built for him by the ubiquitous Nash but refaced with plangent Portland Stone this century, I was definitely in London, but the smell in the air and the sound in my ears was of the northlands of Ontario. The smell was of autumn – clear, crisp, fresh, earthy and wooden. The sound was of chain-saws, which surrounded us as contract tree surgeons dismembered the fallen and attended to the wounded.

Monitored by the video cameras, the dogs investigated vertical plane trees by the **Broad Walk**. Julia leapt on to the trunk of a fallen plane that had been shorn of its branches and scampered back and forth. The dogs tried to climb up with her but fell back and contented themselves with picking up branches and sweeping the paths. Passing tourists smiled and took pictures of the English at play, while Scotland Yard recorded it all for posterity.

Security has been an age-old problem here. Queen Victoria used Broad Walk, this now closed plane-tree-lined carriageway, as her direct access to Piccadilly and at least three attempts on her life were made in Green Park.

A bobby walked past with a measured, nonchalant, 'I'm in no rush – don't get alarmed' stride and at almost the exact site where Sir Robert 'Bobby' Peel, founder of the Metropolitan Police, was fatally injured in a fall from a horse, nodded a greeting to Julia and smiled at the dogs' antics.

We followed the central lime-tree-lined path that descends into a slight dell towards Hyde Park Corner, and watched a springer spaniel in the distance retrieve sticks thrown by his master. The Tyburn, the stream that has its origin back at the ponds on Hampstead Heath and which feeds the lake in Regent's Park, runs diverted in a conduit beneath where we were walking to empty near by into the Thames, but this was the nearest the dogs were going to get to water now. We walked on, Julia and I counting the destruction and the dogs rearranging fallen limbs. Further ahead, near Piccadilly, we saw concentrated canine activity and headed towards it.

A man in a tweed hat, green nylon jacket, Viyella shirt, cravat, pressed jeans and Wellington boots was standing at attention shouting commands to two women with large dogs, a Dobermann and a harlequin Great Dane. The women in turn were issuing commands to their dogs, none of which were seemingly being obeyed. The dogs were far more interested in my salacious gang who were running over to investigate.

Liberty ran at speed towards the dogs, then dropped into an alert sit and observed their reactions. Lexington doddled behind and, on seeing Liberty stop, circled back to us. I walked on to the head of the group and introduced myself, giving my veterinary credentials. His morning class was ending and I was interested in what he was training these dogs and their owners to do.

'These are the worst delinquents I have to contend with and they let their dogs walk all over them,' he replied, grinning with amusement. He enjoyed speaking his mind to a vet.

'Those dogs are a danger in this park, but those women just can't understand they need firm discipline. I spoke to her husband –' he pointed to the woman with the Great Dane – 'and told him that it would be just as useful if we came here, his wife and I, with an empty lead and I taught her how to handle that bitch, but he didn't think he'd be getting his money's worth if we came without the dog. That dog only hinders her training. All she thinks about is whether I'm going to criticise her bloody dog's behaviour. In her eyes it can simply do no wrong. To her, it's an angel, whereas in fact it's a nervous bitch and aggressive because of it.'

I liked his no-nonsense approach and asked him how he handles macho dogs and trains them to the lead.

'We used to call it checking but that upset people, so now I call it conditioning. When the dog lunges forward on its lead, you check it hard enough to throw it into a backward somersault and shout "NO". Dogs are pack animals. They respond to authority.'

'What about biters?' I asked, speculating in my mind that he would be a 'muzzle man'.

'The Yellow Pages technique is best. Especially the Central London Yellow Pages. My assistant has just handled a golden cocker spaniel that bites anyone who comes through the front door of his house. Her vet had told her to teach the bloody dog to sit and stay, to leave its lead attached to it indoors and to stop petting it and only reward it for good behaviour, but these people can't find it in themselves to treat their dogs this way. The vet's in airy-fairy land if he thinks that one of these pet-lovers is going to stop petting her poochie.'

This guy was talking about *me* and he didn't know it. I was the one who had given these instructions!

'We trained this dog in a day not to bite visitors. I told the lady to give me a key to the front door and go shopping for the afternoon and had my assistant visit the house. He went over, unlocked the front door and then rang the doorbell. The dog came flying out at him and he swatted it with the Yellow Pages. Then he shut the door and went around the corner to the café for a cuppa. After his tea, he went back, unlocked the door, rang the bell, waited for the dog to run down the hallway, then threw the door open and bashed the dog with the Yellow Pages again. Off to the café, another cup of tea, then back to the house. The dog came tearing out again and got the Yellow Pages treatment again. The fourth time, my assistant unlocked the door, rang the bell, opened the door and the dog just looked around the corner from the kitchen. No barking – no biting – a complete cure. It took an hour. The owners are delighted. They said that the dog was dividing the family and that their relatives refused to visit them because of the bloody thing.'

'Interesting,' I mumbled. Here was an exercise in the practical versus the theoretical. This man was a pragmatist, but what about the dog's concussed grey matter?

I was rapidly developing a pragmatic interest in this dog-trainer and asked him whether he always used Green Park to train dogs and owners.

'Not always. I was reported to the police in Regent's Park once for "trading" in the park. A lady had a problem with her bulldog. It used to remove any rubber bollards it saw on the street and drag them home. She had a roomful of them and was deeply embarrassed, so my assistant and I went with her to Regent's Park so I could teach her how to check her dog if it was going for a bollard. The trouble was that the dog got hold of a branch, a small log really, and wouldn't let go. I lifted the log and the dog into the air but it still wouldn't let go. It just hung there. My assistant and I took turns holding the log with the dog hanging from it. We did it for forty minutes and it still wouldn't let go.

'The woman finally said that she had to leave to pick her daughter up from school. I couldn't let the dog win, so we walked over to the lake and I dunked the dog in it and it finally released the log, but someone reported us to the police for being cruel to the dog. I used to be with the police so I'm not very impressed with a uniform. I asked the constable whether it was unlawful to have an unruly dog in the park and he said it was. Then I asked him if overcoming that unruliness was a crime. That stymied him, so he went back to basics and just repeated that trading in the Royal Parks is illegal. I don't come here often but the only way to train for some problems is to do the training at the scene of the crime.'

His stories were fascinating, but the dogs were anxious to investigate other realms and Julia's arm was geting tired from throwing sticks. We exchanged telephone numbers and, turning from the Hyde Park Corner end of Green Park, we walked back towards Piccadilly Circus past a line of hawthorns lying like slain giants along the rim. I find it hard to imagine that in my lifetime there was still a haysel on this site each summer and that flocks of sheep here grazed near by in Hyde Park. Sir John Gielgud commented once, when talking to a man who had never visited London, 'Pity you've missed it.' Was it really simply a Gielgudism or rather the lucid truth?

The traffic noise was intense, so we moved slightly deeper into the park coming upon a water fountain, the only statue in the park, a naked lady with a whip flogging a greyhound. I don't know what it means but, perhaps in deference to the implied cruelty, a copper pipe runs from the fountain under the footpath to the base of lamp post number 25 near by, where it empties into a marble drinking trough for dogs. I cleared it of fallen leaves and pointed it out to my twosome who gave peremptory laps and charged on.

By **Green Park** tube station we left this green but battered precinct and crossed **Piccadilly** to **Clarges Street**, heading towards Berkeley Square.

There are prettier streets we could have taken, but Clarges Street is where the canine Somerset House stands, the Kennel Club, where Lib's and Lex's birth certificates are stored on microfiche. It has a modern façade bereft of even the remotest hint of attraction, what I think at one time was called neo-Stalinist in design. We proceeded up this dogless street to **Curzon Street**. Near by, at the foot of Hertford Street near Shepherd Market, once stood a pub called The Dog and Duck. Ducks with tied wings were thrown into the adjacent pond and with either your own dog or a rented one you could bet on which dog would retrieve the most ducks. A consistent winner was a market butcher's toothless cur known as 'The Flying Spaniel'.

Rather than turning left towards Hertford Street we turned right, and two minutes later found ourselves at the bottom of **Berkeley Square**. At one time this was a densely wooded square but by 1935 only thirty-three giant plane trees remained, planted in 1789 by

73

# Walk Four...

Edward Bouverie, a neighbour of the gothic novelist Horace Walpole. Today there were thirty-one trees, two of the giants, the largest plane trees in all of England, having been destroyed by the hurricane. The square was padlocked as City of Westminster workmen removed broken branches dangerously dangling above the pathways, so we walked around the square past Bruton Street where in another age Queen Elizabeth was born but which in a new age housed Julia's hairdresser, and out at the top of **Davies Street**. Nightingales didn't sing, nor perhaps have they ever. Eric Maschewitz got his idea for his ageless love song from a schmaltzy short story written by Michael Arlen in the 1920s. The nearest that nightingales have ever been is probably Keats' garden back up in Hampstead.

From Davies Street, we turned left into **Mount Street** and right into **Carlos Place** before arriving at **Grosvenor Square**, which seemed to have survived the gale almost unscathed, the only damage appearing to be at the south-west corner in front of the brooding monolithic American Embassy. The dogs were delighted to be freed from their leads and trotted about giving friendly hellos to passers-by and other dogs. A Labrador was being marched, under escort, out of the far side of this open six-acre patch of green, while a Cavalier King Charles, obviouslyy the dog of the moment in this part of London, carried out perfunctory nasal investigations of the rubbish bins. Three men stood talking to a dark haired woman who was throwing a tennis ball for her Yorkie to fetch. On the north side of the square, a small black and tan mongrel ran in circles by the statue of Franklin Roosevelt.

'Hi,' the men said as we smiled and passed by.

'Hi,' we replied, getting into the swing of things.

With the Americans at one end of the square and Canadian High Commission offices at the other, this was a real slice of transplanted North America.

Grosvenor Square has always had American connections, from the time that their first Ambasador and future president John Adams took up residence at number 6 in 1786. Wealthy Americans followed – Astors and Pierpont Morgans – but today their equivalents prefer Belgravia. Although some Americans still live around the square, it is primarily peopled by affluent Greek and Arab families.

I made my way over towards the elegant-looking dark-haired woman dressed like a successful Mayfair businesswoman in navy blues, with a flash of colour provided by her paisley pattern cashmere shawl. Her Yorkshire terrier thought it was a Yorkshire retriever and was expectantly returning a tossed tennis ball with the aplomb of a springer spaniel.

'How did you train him to do it?' I asked.

'It's quite simple. I treat Pip as I would a first-year university student. I told him that if he wanted me to throw the ball then he would have to return it.'

As we talked, the American male congregation asked in turn if they could throw the ball, which they did, covering their palms in the process with Pip saliva. Julia walked Liberty and Lexington off to Roosevelt so they would not interfere.

'I used to exercise Pip in Hyde Park but we left because of a few nasty incidents with Rottweilers. The terrible thing is that Pip was savaged by an old English sheepdog in here.'

Pip continued to race like an overwound toy, making barking elliptical charges at a sheepdog and the Cavalier as they walked past, then returned the disgusting ball to his mistress who handed it to one of her American quorum who threw it for her. Her dog was genuinely amazing – a crowd-stopper.

'American or Canadian?' one of the group asked.

I replied the latter but went on to explain that I was impressed by the Mayfair businesswoman's dog and that this wasn't just a simple compliment. This was a *veterinary* compliment.

'Vet, huh?' replied the oldest member of the quorum, a silver-haired rotund man with grey faded eyes. 'J'ever hear about the night the French Ambassador's dog died in Washington? Henri Bonnet was the Ambassador and he was holding an important dinner for John Foster Dulles, who was then our Secretary of State. Bonnet wanted something extra special so he had some truffles flown in specially from France. When they arrived the chef gave them to Bonnet, who sniffed them and thought they were a bit high, so they gave one to his dog who seemed to enjoy it enormously and decided to serve them that evening. The dinner went fine but when they were well along to the cheese, the butler came in pale-faced, see, and handed Bonnet a note which read, "The dog just died."

'Well, Bonnet being a consummate diplomat, excused himself from the table and phoned his doctor. I mean, could you see the papers the next day? "French Poison Secretary of State." So the doctor rushed over with emetic pills. Bonnet returned to the table and rather *en passant* mentioned that some people are sensitive to truffles and that his dog, with whom he had shared these truffles, had just died, but that he had taken the precaution of obtaining some emetic pills and these were available for anyone who wanted them.

'Well, all the guests grabbed them. The senior ranking guests and ladies were allowed to use the bathrooms and the others went out and puked in the garden. The group finally reconvened and over cognac and coffee one of the guests asked Bonnet whether his dog suffered unduly.

'He didn't know but thought it was a good question and asked the chef. "Did he take long to die?" he asked.

'"Not at all, Monsieur l'Ambassadeur,' his chef replied. 'The truck 'it 'im squarely and broke 'is neck."

'Cyrus Sulzberger, the foreign correspondent on *The New York Times*, told me that story and I've been dying to tell it to a vet for years,' he added, grinning broadly, and with that he excused himself and walked back towards his embassy.

I threw the ball once more for Pip, then rejoined Julia by the Roosevelt statue.

'Watch this,' she said and, having me stand well in front of FDR, she marched Liberty over to the concrete plinth to the left of the steps leading up to the President and had her jump up and sit on it. She then led Lexington to the plinth to the right and had her jump up and sit on that, instructing both dogs to stay. FDR guarded by dogs rampant. It looked idiotic, but the lunchtime visitors found it as benignly funny as we did.

The dogs were released from their 'hold' and trotted over to the fountain and pool to the left where, by the words 'Freedom from Want' and 'Freedom from Fear', they stood on their hind legs and drooped their bodies over the pool edge to lap from the water below. A trail of water led from the fountain across to a rubbish bin filled with sticks, undoubtedly left there by the Labrador I had seen leaving the square twenty minutes earlier.

We gathered up the dogs and walked them to the north-west gate of the square and then, with their leads reapplied, marched off along **Upper Brook Street** towards **Park Lane**. There we took the malodorous underpass to **Hyde Park** and entered by **Brook Gate**. Both dogs surreptitiously headed off towards the Serpentine. They were back on their own territory and knew it, but I headed them off before they reached the reservoir. Another swim would have to wait until tomorrow.

# Walk Five

## Hyde Park to Battersea Park

START: Cumberland Gate (Marble Arch) entrance to Hyde Park, W1.

END: Chelsea Bridge entrance to Battersea Park, SW11.

LENGTH: Approximately 6½ miles.

TIME: Approximately 3¾ hours.

LEADS: Required in ornamental gardens of Kensington Gardens, gardens of the Imperial College of Science and Technology and on Royal Avenue.

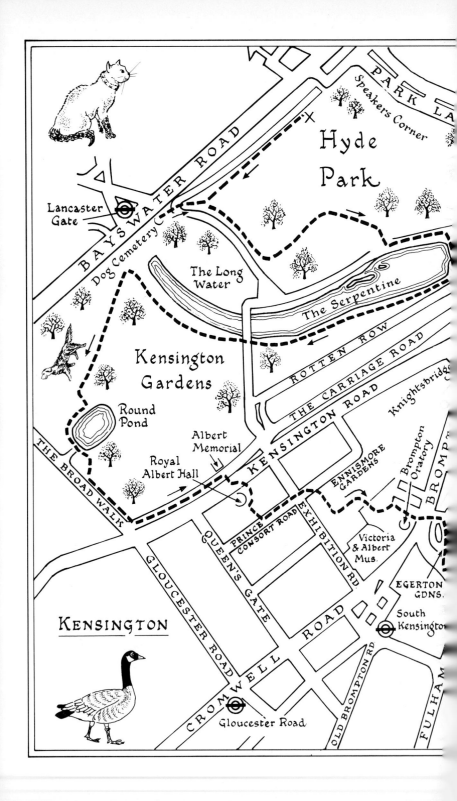

PICCADILLY

CONSTITUTION HILL

SBRIDGE

Hyde Park
Corner

GROSVENOR PLACE

BELGRAVIA

→ Route of walk

Scale

| 0 | ¼ | ½ mile |

| 0 | ½ | 1 Km |

PIMLICO

OANE STREET

Sloane
Square

PIMLICO ROAD

OTT AV.

KINGS RD.

E AVENUE

ELYSTAN
PLACE

ROYAL
AVE.

KING'S ROAD

ORMOND
GDNS.

St LEONARD'S
TERRACE

ROYAL

HOSPITAL ROAD

Burton's
Court

TITE ST.

CHELSEA BRIDGE RD.

Ranelagh Gardens

Royal
Hospital

CHELSEA EMBANKMENT

GROSVENOR RD.

CHELSEA BR.

River Thames

PMc

# Walk Five...

## From Hyde Park, through Kensington Gardens
## to Battersea Park

Evelyn Waugh once commented that the streets of London, 'once one of the splendours of Europe, are now only fit as promenades of pet dogs'. He might as well have been speaking of Hyde Park.

King Henry VIII seized the land from the Church and enclosed it with a wall. King George II's wife Caroline had the Westbourne dammed to create the forty acres of the Serpentine and Long Water, something for which my dogs and many more are eternally grateful. In Queen Victoria's reign, Hyde Park became part of the 'London Season'. It was a verdant backdrop for wealth and ostentation. The first occupants of the park between seven and ten in the morning were 'judges, barristers, surgeons, physicians, actors, writers, African millionaires and German Jews' who, according to Mrs Alex Tweedie, a park biographer of the time, would take their exercise there then return to their homes for bath and breakfast before settling down to the Law Courts, Chambers or the consulting-room for the rest of the day. As they departed, the park was given over to aristocratic babies and their nurses. By noon the babes had retired, replaced by older children with their governesses. In late summer afternoon, from five until seven, the fashionable would drive through Hyde Park, often four or five carriages abreast, moving at a snail's pace from Hyde Park Corner to Knightsbridge Barracks or, later on, more fashionably, to Marble Arch. Finally, between six and seven o'clock, the Queen, in her royal carriage – a high barouche with red wheels – would ride through and her subjects would raise their hats or curtsey as her carriage passed by at an ordinary trot.

It is a far cry from the Hyde Park of today. Flocks of migrant gulls, born in Scandinavia and the Baltic, rested on the sodden ground above the Metropolitan Police underground car pound. It was early morning, another lustreless grey and moody day and we were standing at the Cumberland Gate entrance to Hyde Park. There wasn't a barrister or surgeon in sight, only a man in his late twenties in expensive casuals racing back with his rough collie to his Porsche, parked on the ring road, where a motorcycle policeman was sternly waiting. Two mounted police cantered by on the bridle path, but Liberty and Lexington were too far away to notice the canine gifts their fellow quadrupeds were discharging.

Hyde Park was devastated. The hurricane damage had been far worse here than in St James's Park or Green Park. Entire rows of trees lay in geometric lines, their leaves not yet dying, still curiously alive. They lay across virtually every tarmacked footpath and across the bridlepath too, forcing both walkers and riders to divert over the waterlogged grass.

'I know it's dreadful to say, but it will be so boring when it's all tidied up,' was Julia's comment.

The dogs both nodded their heads as if in agreement with this thought then raced off looking for action. By now the motorcycle cop had moved on down the road and was remonstrating with a cabbie who was cleaning his windows.

In the very early morning, between 7.45 and 8.45, Hyde Park is teeming with dogs and their owners on short purposeful walks – morning saunters to prepare the dogs for their daily incarcerations in their luxury gaolhouses while their masters and mistresses go off to work. We had missed these. Only two Yorkies came in sight. Oblivious to their mistress's encouragements, one looked for slugs in the damp grass as the other carried out chemical analyses of the earth with its mouth. Both bounced into life and tried to eat my retrievers as they passed but both Lib and Lex looked upon their behaviour as nothing more than an intemperate joke. Julia in the meantime was rolling logs into a pile. 'It's such a waste. This will make marvellous firewood.'

She was right, only our fire at home is a gas log fire.

We continued walking westwards through the park, paralleling Bayswater Road, and the dogs cavorted through the trees. Their mark is etched on every blade of grass here.

As the dogs played hide and seek amongst the branches of the prostrate planes, Julia pointed out two large dogs further ahead. Both were retrieving their chain leads being thrown by their masters. A Ford van with a fluorescent orange stripe on it was parked near by. They were obviously police dogs on their tea break, so we changed direction and walked towards them.

Libby has always had a penchant for slightly mean-looking dogs, the canine equivalent of Hell's Angels, and this German shepherd fitted the bill. His coat was rather dull and bristly, reddened in an almost sunburnt way through constant outdoor exposure in the previous months. He was slightly swaybacked and he was *big*. He looked like he hadn't shaved for a week.

A flight of Canada geese passed low overhead, a noisy gaggle heading in the direction of Selfridges, but the dogs were oblivious to them. Lib raced forward and, as the shepherd's handler saw her coming, he slipped his lead on his dog and commanded him to sit. Lib raced up to the shepherd and then ten feet away instantly stopped and sat sphinx-like, staring him in the eye and wagging her tail.

'Hi!' she was saying. 'I'm a salacious bitch. No aggro. Wanna play games?'

Most dogs are skilful at innately understanding this body language and I spoke to the handler, a rather corpulent, bearded man with a ruddy complexion and friendly smile, telling him that Lib was good at defusing potentially dangerous situations. He slackened his hold on his dog and allowed him to sniff Lib.

The shepherd's initial interest was sex but Lib coyly swirled in the air, barked and told him that she was spayed and no longer interested in sex.

'Let's play tag,' she implored with her body language.

The dog's rather massive handler was still slightly ill at ease over letting his dog off 'hold', so I explained that I was a vet and would patch up whoever needed it. He laughed and removed the choke from his brute, who instantly dived on Lexington's bum. She'd been observing it all from behind Julia. Lex rolled over cowering but Liberty raced in and with a tease convinced the shepherd that she was more fun. They ran off.

'I don't see many guard dogs in my practice,' I said to the shepherd's handler, passing the time.

'Please don't call them "guard dogs". These dogs spend their time walking the streets or in classrooms full of children being petted. They don't really do any guarding at all.'

I asked why the Met only uses German shepherds.

'We've got a bouvier. The French police use them, so we tried them, but they're too stubborn. The last bouvier in the Met will be retired soon when his handler retires. We tried Rottweilers, but they're too hard. We tried Dobermanns but they're too flighty. They're all good in one way or another but not as all-rounders. We need all-purpose dogs, dogs that will scent, protect or attack on command, and there's still nothing better than a shepherd.'

I've been involved with a charity that trains dogs for deaf people. The first dogs we trained were gifts from the public but we had a few unexpected behavioural problems, so I asked him where his dog came from.

'He came from a pub. He was a right pig! He wouldn't do anything for me but I could see that he'd be a good police dog.'

I looked at him, a big, mean nasty-looking dog lording it over Lib who was loving it all, and understood what he meant.

'It took a long time for me to gain his confidence, but he's been magnificent. He's found people in amazing places for me and has saved me four times since I've had him. Once I was alone with him and faced with thirty to forty hooligans. I was scared stiff and all he wanted to do was take them all on. He gave me courage. When it was all over a child could have stroked him and he'd love it. We've got 350 dogs in the Met and we're breeding around sixty a year now. The problem with dogs that are given as gifts is that they're dogs that the owners can't handle. Lots of them are pigs like him. The problem with breeding our own is we have to breed them down, breed more gentle dogs and I don't know if that's a good thing.'

I said that I'd heard the Swedish police train their dogs not to 'attack' but to 'retrieve', not to bite and chew but to grab and return.

'That's basically what we do. We start training them with a false arm, a cricket bat wrapped in padding inside a sleeve. You throw the arm and train the dog to return it. Once he's fully trained, you graduate to the bite suit and train the dog to grab the arm and drag the villain back to the handler. The dogs and handlers get sixteen weeks of basic training, then we all go back each year for a four-week refresher.'

By now his dog and Liberty were back beside us. Looking at the shepherd more closely I could see that he had badly chewed the hair around the base of his tail, a common sign of anal gland irritation, and that his coat was not simply dull from summer exposure but was listless in the way that shepherds' coats become if they aren't well nourished. I asked what happens when the dogs reach retirement.

'We're allowed to keep them or they're put down. Almost every-one keeps his old dog and at the same time you've got the new pup in your home. You get the new pup when it's ten weeks old and take him everywhere – cellars, steps, on the tube, through traffic. That way he grows up frightened of nothing. I'm looking forward to the new pup but hope he'll be less of a pig than this one. Tell me something, my dog's got a pancreas problem – that's why his coat is so godawful – and I give him six capsules of pig pancreas every day. The Met supplies these now but I'll have to do that when he retires. Is there anything else I can do?'

That was the explanation for the dull coat, simple pancreas insufficiency, and I explained costs and alternatives to him.

While I talked, Julia assuaged Lexington and gathered bundles of branches. Her pockets bulged with fallen acorns. I expected her to have them in her cheek pouches too. The other police dog and handler had been in their van all this time and now the other dog was barking, so I wished them good luck and Lib and I returned to the others and continued towards **Victoria Gate**.

The park was filling with the later Sunday morning crowd. An American lady jogged by accompanied by an elderly German shepherd that was obviously not enjoying the event. An elderly man in dirty well-worn black shoes and unwashed clothes sat on a park bench brushing a black and white mutt. I could see two Staffordshire bull terriers and, more unusually, a soft-coated wheaten terrier.

'Look! There's another hat!' Julia cried, eyeing a large-rimmed orange felt headpiece on a passing Yorkie walker. 'You don't often meet hats.'

Julia lives her life in hats. I wake up in the morning to a blonde head surmounted, no, actually enveloped in some Peruvian Indian's bowler. She fries eggs wearing a homburg. She paints wearing a sombrero. She bathes in a Panama. My daughters now do the same.

At Victoria Gate we crossed **The Ring** so that I could show Julia the dog cemetery. Technically, it's not just a dog cemetery. From 1880 for the next forty-odd years, it became the final resting place of around two hundred pets, including birds, cats and monkeys. I had been allowed into it one day in 1986 after it had been tidied, and was taken by the names of these pets. They were almost all monosyllabic: Chum, Turk, Flo, Spot, Ruff, Floss, Bones, Gyp, Wisp, Drag, Snap, Fluff, Scoop, Chips, Flick, Tar, Mouse. The polysyllabic names were equally simple: Bogie, Joker, Runty, Fairy, Curly, Nigger, Nipper, Butcha, Bunta. Prince, Marine Commando of Anisor, aged eleven years, is buried here, as is 'Dear Little Gyp' and 'Darling Boss'.

This little cemetery exemplifies two facets of our relationship with pets. The loss that pet-owners feel today when their pets die isn't unique. The Victorians felt the same emptiness as we do when their pets died, and memorialised their loss through ritual, by burying their pets here. The names, however, are vastly different.

One hundred years ago a dog was given a dog's name. Spot. Nipper. Chum. Bones. Bones! That's a great name. I wish I'd thought of that for one of my dogs. That's a *real* dog's name. Today, pets are much more members of the family, perhaps even people substitutes in some ways. Ben and Sally are the most popular names for dogs in Britain today. The only dogs that, as a general rule, are still routinely given dog names are the big defence breeds, the Princes, Dukes, Sabres and Vulcans.

I used to think that pet cemeteries were the ultimate symbol of a society gone slightly mad. After my years in practice, however, after years of observing the sadness that owners feel when their pets die, I've changed my tune. People need ritual and custom, and burial is a standard Western ritual. Private burial in your own garden is in most cases illegal and that leaves the pet cemetery as one of the only viable alternatives. I wouldn't bury my own dogs in one but no longer do I condemn those who do.

The dog cemetery is locked to casual visitors, but before retracing our steps across The Ring, Julia walked me down to a massive hawthorn that had fallen across the road and been cleared to the side.

'I want it.'

'Why?' I countered.

'Why, for the lounge.'

The tree was eighty feet tall and had a girth that would need two people to put their arms around.

'Not all of it,' she continued. 'Just a slive. Near the bottom. For a table.'

I pointed out the logistic difficulties in preparing a slice. It was too thick for a chain-saw to slice through in one go and, besides, a decent slice would weigh hundreds of pounds.

'OK. Then this,' she replied, singling out a two-foot-long log almost eighteen inches in diameter. I can use this as a planter.'

It is now in our kitchen, all two hundred pounds of it. I hope the Department of the Environment is pleased with our public-spirited help in tidying the park. My back, on the other hand, is not!

Back in the main part of the park, more dogs were congregating. Most were big dogs, a Dobermann, a Labrador and others that looked similar to these but were the results of unauthorised assignations. We walked through the centre of the park towards the police station and ranger's lodge. Gunter, a massive Rottweiler pup, sloped over to play but was instantly recalled by his owner.

The giant plane tree to the north of the police station had come down in the storm, crushing to a pulp the grey Jaguar on the drive of the adjacent cottage. The deceased car was covered in a green tarpaulin shroud and, as if in revenge, the tree had been completely dismembered, each piece of the trunk cut and numbered, left like a pile of fallen ruins in a Greek temple, awaiting restoration elsewhere. Julia counted the rings on the stump. There were 110. The neighbouring hawthorns, a third the size of the plane, each had eighty-eight rings. It was fascinating to be able to date so accurately the trees, to know exactly when they had been planted, but the sadness at the overwhelming destruction was greater.

As we continued, the head of the nursery walked past. I knew him through his cats and we paused to talk. Over 700 trees were felled in the storm in Hyde Park and Kensington Gardens, he told us. The squirrels disappeared for two days before re-emerging to survey the damage. The hedgehogs, on the other hand, were there, even at the height of the storm, awaiting their nightly drink of milk.

From a veterinary viewpoint, hedgehogs are amazing. Nothing seems to disturb them. If during winter the weather gets too cold, they simply pump out a little extra of their own anti-freeze which prevents their blood from clotting and go off for a meal. Even sex, which when you think of it, might be a bit uncomfortable for the male, is no big deal. They've simply got extra long willies.

'The saddest thing for me is that the tawny owl that lived in the conifer next to the police stables hasn't been heard since the storm,' the nurseryman continued, and I brought my thoughts back to the matter in hand.

As far as the other wildlife was concerned, everything was virtually back to normal. During the past winter he had had a problem with a fox entering the nurseries. It had been taking ornamental fowl from the Serpentine but hadn't been seen for some time now. I was surprised that there was a fox in the heart of London.

'There are probably over 3,000 foxes in the old GLC area,' he told me. 'There used to be a fox that lived in Holland Park that would make its way from there, through Kensington Gardens and past where we are standing now, to Hyde Park Corner, where it took the pedestrian underpass as a shortcut to Green Park then into St James's Park where it fed on the ducks. Some mornings you could still smell its scent in the underpass. No. Foxes are everywhere.'

I shouldn't really have been surprised. Foxes will go wherever there's a meal. In the Arctic, foxes live hundreds of miles out on the sea ice, completely dependent for their food on leftovers from polar bear kills.

'What about rabbits?' I asked. After all, since their introduction to England by the Normans, rabbits have been the bane of the nurseryman's life.

'Strangely, we've found a natural method of controlling rabbits in the park. The gamekeeper has to shoot dozens of squirrels each year, but feral cats are taking care of the rabbits. The only rabbits presently here are in the beds near Hyde Park Corner and their numbers are well under control. People have released their cats in the park. People release the strangest things. We were inundated last year with cocks and hens that someone was buying, 'rescuing', in their minds, from some street market and dumping in here. Confucius was the first cat to develop a taste for rabbits. We called her Confucius because you could talk to her in Chinese and she understood. Confucius had a son, Mr Bruiser, who's now eleven years old, and he mated with another wild she-cat. Three of that brood now live in the nursery. The fourth one was kicked by a horse in the stables and died. One of that brood, Beasty Boy, is the best rabbiter, but he drags their bodies back to the nursery and eats them there, head and all.'

My dogs listened gape-mouthed. They drooled at the good fortune these cats had encountered and immediately offered their services to the Department of the Environment as unpaid game-keepers, squirrel division.

The hurricane had wrought devastation on Hyde Park but had fortunately spared some of the unique trees. The Chinese varnish tree, the evergreen magnolia and the bean tree, the nurseryman explained, all by the nursery where we were standing, had been saved. We thanked him for his explanations and continued walking south towards the **Serpentine**, past a couple in country casuals, fashionable tweeds and sensible shoes walking two Cavalier King Charles spaniels and a slinking Siamese cat. Julia shouted to me to keep Libby away from the cat but both dogs were oblivious to everything but the water. They had smelt it and were racing to it.

'If you shake on me you're never coming here again,' Julia shouted after the dogs, so they shook on a group of German tourists instead. We caught up with them as Lexington swam lengths and Libby raced in a sine wave along the embankment, in and out of the water, stopping occasionally to investigate the ground. It was swan droppings – even better than goose droppings.

'Liberty, stoppit! No wonder I never come here,' fumed the commander.

Julia simply can't abide the ancient and hallowed canine custom of eating droppings. I once wrote a chapter in a book about that behaviour especially for her. She might not believe me if I tell her why a dog behaves that way, but she might believe what she reads!

The dog's boss grabbed both dogs by their collars and force-marched them around the eastern end of the Serpentine to the southern side where fishermen were vainly hoping to pull something in. If they had been fishing here in the early 1800s they might have caught more than they bargained for. When the Serpentine was drained and cleaned in the mid-1800s, hundreds of baby skeletons were found.

Until that time the Serpentine had been fed by the Westbourne. Queen Charlotte, who created the revolutionary 'serpentine' design, kept her pet swan, 'Jack' here. He was obviously a miserable old swan and killed many birds and dogs before being pecked to death by a pack of Polish geese. Today the Serpentine receives fresh water from artestian wells on Duck Island in St James's Park. The water is pumped from St James's to the Round Pond in Kensington Gardens and then returns by gravity down to the Serpentine, on to the lake behind Buckingham Palace and finally back to the lake in St James's Park. The Westbourne, in the meantime, encased in iron, bypasses these bodies of water and travels through conduits down to the Thames. You can see the conduit in Sloane Square tube station where it passes over the heads of passengers awaiting their trains.

A man with three cocker spaniels trotted by. Two of his dogs were carrying sticks in their mouths until my dogs relieved them of their treasures. Both continued their water antics as we passed the island in the Serpentine. Kingfishers now nest in the sandbar there, a welcome return to central London. Other previous losses are less likely to be overcome. Kites were at one time plentiful in London. They were almost pet-like scavengers, but the last kite to nest in London nested in a tree near this spot in 1826 and gulls and pigeons have filled the ecological niche left by the metropolis's original feathered scavengers. Only a short time later, the last deer in the park were transferred, in 1831, to Richmond Park. Until that time, the Spanish, French, Venetian and Dutch ambassadors had the right to kill a brace of bucks a year with hounds. The reason why the deer were moved was because of the number of pet dogs being killed by gamekeepers for worrying the deer.

We walked past the Lido. Rare gannets and razorbills have been seen here. The water is oxygenated to keep it pure for swimming and this undoubtedly makes it a great place to go fishing if you're a water bird. In October, when there is no swimming, it also provides a safe haven for more timid birds.

As we approached the pass under the bridge leading into Kensington Gardens, Lexington once more took to water and swam out to investigate some Canada geese. Water is some dogs' natural habitat and that happens to be the case with Lex. For her there is an unmitigated joy that comes from a swim. I can't help but think it's the same joy that people who like swimming also have – the weightlessness, the silken glide, the sensuous feeling of being incorporated in water. Do dogs subconsciously yearn to return to the womb?

We entered **Kensington Gardens**, which had previously been closed to the public for two weeks after the hurricane. The devastation, if anything, was worse than in Hyde Park if only because there are so many more trees here. Again, it was the London planes, heavy with leaf, that had suffered most severely. Some limes were down and both sweet and horse chestnut and oaks suffered limb losses, but the planes were ravaged. The sound of their falling must have been magnificent!

Hyde Park and Kensington Gardens together form the classic English city green space. You simply know you can be nowhere else in the world when you are here, but it's curious how so few of the trees that invest this feeling are native to the British Isles. The sweet chestnut was introduced into Britain by the Romans, but the horse chestnut, from Northern Greece, didn't arrive for another 1,500 years. The common lime tree is really a hybrid originally from Flanders and the avuncular London plane is a hybrid between an oriental plane and an American buttonwood tree, which were accidentally crossed in Oxford in 1690.

No one can recall a storm with such savagery as the one we suffered just before this walk, but there have without doubt been storms of equal destruction in times past. There was one shortly after the Norman Conquest, in 1091, in which a great gale from the south-east unroofed most of London's churches and blew down over 600 houses. The fallen trees in front of us all lay in a north-easterly line, yielding to a similar wind.

Although the day remained deeply overcast, with rain threatening to inundate us any minute, the Gardens were filled with people, mostly nearby residents with children or pets. There were few tourists and no sign of the groups of extended Arab families that give the park the feel of an oriental bazaar in high summer.

By now, both dogs were back in the water, swimming quite illegally as it is signposted that dogs must not disturb the ducks and geese. I allowed it because my dogs always leave the game alone. If they had the ability to do so, they should consider themselves lucky to be in the Gardens in the first place, let alone in the water. It wasn't until well into Queen Victoria's reign that dogs (or even working people or servants in livery, for that matter) were even allowed in the place.

The dogs ran out, shook themselves, rolled on the grass, then hared off up the hill. Julia shouted a command and they returned directly, sitting loyally for her, looking at her with pleading, sorrowful eyes, awaiting her instructions.

'If you race around you'll have your leads put back on. WALK!'

And they did.

We passed Peter Pan, who should really be the patron saint of dogs. Finches, sparrows, starlings and tits muttered in the trees surrounding the statue enclosure while Canada geese and mallards hung about in the water keenly observing human behaviour.

Most of the pet-owners we have met so far on our walk probably think of their dogs as I used to and still do think of Peter Pan. My Peter Pan isn't a child. He might look like a child, but he's a guide and protector, a watch dog. After all, even Captain Hook is no match for Peter. Peter doesn't have to conform to the constraints of culture, either. He's a free spirit, a force of nature. He almost understands and feels the tug of human emotions but ultimately gives in to his instinct to be a free spirit. That's how so many people feel about their dogs, even if only in a subliminal way. Dogs are like Peter Pan, caught between nature and culture. They never grow up and we don't expect them to. They are unchanging in an ever-changing world. Our children evolve from a total dependency upon us through the first pangs or delight at the realisation that they are independent beings and then in adolescence through the programmed rebellion, however mild it may be, that is necessary for them to break bonds and become self-fulfilled individuals who then repeat the exercise for the next generation. These natural stages can be painful. After all, we all like to maintain the status quo. In our relationships with pets we *do* maintain the status quo. Pets remain, like Peter Pan, unchanging, constant, a rock. Peter Pan will never grow up and neither will our pets. For better or worse, we humans are invested with a life-long parenting instinct. We have a biologically engined need to nurture. That's why so many of us do such a dumb thing and get such great emotional rewards from keeping pets.

Rather than walk to the fountains near Lancaster Gate, we turned left towards **Speke's Monument**. The ground was littered with felled trees, fallen branches, leaves coloured from canary yellow through gold to rust, and shells of myriads of chestnuts.

Julia looked incredulous. 'Not a single chestnut. It's disgraceful of those squirrels when you think of how many nuts there are.'

What she didn't know and I wasn't going to tell her now was the field day dogs were having in catching these overburdened rodents. One client of mine, whose whippet caught and killed four pot-bellied squirrels in one day, put her dog on a low dose of valium for a few days, simply to slow it down a little, not because she finds her pet's blood lust offensive but simply because of the verbal abuse she was receiving from observers of her dog's behaviour.

Rain started falling, so we walked on directly to the **Round Pond**, pausing on the way for me to scratch at two different types of lichen on a marker stone. Lichens only grow in pure air, and the more there are the cleaner the air, so this was an interesting sign of the air quality in London. Somewhere near the pond is a covered well devoted to St Gover, a sixth-century hermit who lived here, but the rain dampened my desire to look for it. Around the pond, the best place in London to observe the workings of water dogs, were a briard, an old English sheepdog, and six mutts. A nanny was imploring Billy a Dalmatian to drop his stick, while James a cocker spaniel, retrieved his from the water. Two border terriers, Sam and George, were being beckoned as the rain was increasing.

'This is where William and Harry come to play,' recounted Julia.

'Which are they?' I asked and got lacerated by her laser vision for my ignorance of the activities of the Royal Family.

Positively zillions of Canada geese paddled about in the foetid opalescent water. Too many. Libby eyed their earthbound droppings.

'Watchit!' the commander enjoined, and Lib skulked away, hanging her head hound-like.

Lex eyed a deckchair floating half submerged in the water and dived in to save it. At the turn of the century there were over 35,000 deckchairs in these parks and queues of people to use them on weekends. This chair unfortunately did not want to be saved. As she grabbed it in her mouth and turned to swim to the shore, it folded over on itself and closed on her, forcing her underwater. She scrambled out from under, frightened at the resistance that the chair had given her and powerstroked herself back to the embankment where she ran to Julia, shook herself, then stood on her hind legs, describing every horrible detail of what had just happened.

'Now, now. There, there.'

If Julia had had a plaster in her pocket she would have put it on Lex to make her feel better.

The rain continued to descend and as we were prepared with neither raincoats nor umbrellas I wondered whether we should simply walk home, only twenty minutes away. Liberty had other plans. A black German shepherd, hackles raised and ears alert, was chasing her and she was loving it. She hared in a zigzag catch-me-if-you-can fashion, always keeping six feet ahead of the charging dog. Another Hell's Angel. She loved it.

'Do you recognise her?' asked her owner. 'That's Arabella. You delivered her. Mr Peeps! Come here at once!'

A shaggy Disney-type dog obediently trotted to her side and was joined by a Yorkshire terrier. 'That's Folly.'

A Gordon setter appeared from nowhere, then a border terrier and a Cavalier King Charles spaniel. 'Hello, William. Hello, Sophie. Hello, Jack.'

She knew them all and they adored her.

Liberty, Lexington and Arabella joined the pack and they all sniffed each other's ears, lip folds and bums. Caroline was a dog-walker. The first three dogs were hers and, although I didn't know her, she remembered me as the vet who had delivered Arabella, one of a litter of ten from a refined and elegant black bitch. The others were her charges, all off their leads, in love with Caroline and firmly under her control.

An excited Labrador joined the gang. 'Now behave, Samson. I'll see you tomorrow.'

Samson's owner appeared and chatted with Caroline, who duly examined Samson's eye. Most vets in London have 'tame' dog-walkers, women who walk the dogs of owners who are either too busy or too lazy to do it themselves. I have one north of the parks and Caroline works the area to the south of the parks. These women share common characteristics. First of all they have an almost innate understanding of canine behaviour, which is why they are so good at what they do. They can walk half a dozen dogs at a time, off their leads, knowing that pack instinct will keep them together as long as the walker has had time to teach her charges that she is the paramount and unquestioned leader. The women are usually single, separated or divorced. I only know of one male dog-walker. And finally, they aren't the meticulous sort. Dog-walkers don't spend their spare time at hairdressers or in front of mirrors. They are really earthy country folk who, through accidents of fate, find themselves mired in the aspic of city life.

As we talked, two handsome black Labradors joined the gang, accompanied by their bemused owner, a dignified man well dressed for a long dog walk in the rain with his Viyella shirt, ascot, corduroy trousers, Barbour coat and a Sony discman surreptitiously peeking from under his scarf. One Lab had a red collar, the other was dressed in blue.

'I've been thinking of getting a golden retriever. Marvellous dogs,' he said to me as he watched Lexington plough whale-like into the Round Pond. I concurred and we watched his dogs enter the water while Lib tried to sniff their tails, then all emerged to chase Arabella.

'What a marvellous life it must be to be a well-cared-for dog. I don't recognise your dogs. Do you live near by?'

Caroline trotted off with her dogs and I continued talking to Mr Labradors. The rain was thinning and Julia and I had decided to continue our walk. The Labs' owner was a research scientist, a Brazilian doctor who had never practised clinical medicine but rather had become intrigued with the neurological mechanisms involved in night vision. He had a research station in Manaus on the Amazon, but had been in London for some time now. Robbie, his stockier dog, was from the Sandilands line of Labradors, a dog out of Queen Elizabeth's kennels.

'I could never use dogs in research. You understand them too well. At one time I was obliged to use monkeys but hated it. You can become just as attached to them.'

I asked him what type of animals he does use.

'South American rodents. Agoutis. Pacas. Coypus. They are fascinating animals but fortunately it is more difficult to form a relationship with them. I have a friend in California with racoons. Now, those are interesting animals because of their humour.'

I asked which was his favourite research animal and why.

'Oh, undoubtedly the paca. It might sound terribly crude, but the paca is the tastiest of all animals.' Our eyes wandered to our mutual pets. 'Dogs are as well cared for as children here, but it is not like that everywhere,' he said with a sardonic smile and a slightly pained weariness in his voice. 'Children in most parts of Brazil are not as well cared for as these dogs.'

It was an uncomfortable thought administered by a considerate and knowledgeable man. We exchanged names and addresses, then Julia and I and our cosseted charges proceeded briskly down **The Broad Walk** towards the dog fountain by Kensington Road, on the site of the aborted dog loo of the 1970s. The dogs were waterlogged from their swimming and we had been walking now for over three hours, so we continued unceremoniously along the bottom of the park, past **Queen's Gate** to the **Albert Memorial**, where leads were placed on the dogs and we 'deparked'. The dogs had had a glorious walk. They had gone swimming and eaten goose and swan droppings to their hearts' content.

'If Liberty stinks tonight, we'll know why,' Julia stated, forgetting that whatever is eaten doesn't disturb the bowels for some time.

When Lib was a pup she leapt up to Julia in excitement one day and swallowed her diamond ear ring. For the next thirty-six hours I collected and X-rayed each stool that passed until I found the missing gem, learning at the same time the exact length of time that an object takes to travel from one orifice to the other!

Having crossed **Kensington Gore**, we were around the back of the Royal Albert Hall now, by the almond trees. Here we met a black and tan mutt that wanted to play, but we marched the dogs on, left on to **Prince Consort Road** then a short right on **Exhibition Road** and left into the gardens of the **Imperial College of Science and Technology**. Not a tree was lost here but a cat was and signs were posted giving its description.

The exit at the bottom left-hand corner of the gardens looks like an entrance to the student accommodation, but a hidden path leads out past the bijoux homes in **Ennismore Gardens Mews** to the gardens behind the **Brompton Oratory**. Only one tree was felled here, a plane. I suspected divine intervention.

A clumber spaniel sauntered, as well as a clumber can saunter, over to my bitches.

'He lika the girls,' said his toothy, compact middle-aged Italian mistress. 'He no lika noisy kids.'

I looked around and didn't see any. After wiping a little pus from his droopy eyelids, we walked on, across **Brompton Road** and through **Egerton Terrace** and past the pumpkin-encrusted homes of **Egerton Gardens**, the seasonal Hallowe'en insignia signifying that this was an American enclave.

'Vanessa Redgrave and Tony Richardson lived here,' Julia explained.

The short strip of **Brompton Road** between Egerton Gardens and Sloane Avenue is today's Mecca for the fashionably wealthy. The Porsche showroom has a brilliantly mirrored sloped ceiling. Les Especialités St Quentin, *'patisserie, traiteur, charcuterie, vins'*, can tickle the most jaded palate. Battalions of double-parked Golfs and Saab turbos lined the street in front of Katherine Hamnett, Domus and Joseph.

Rather than walk down Sloane Avenue we turned left on to **Walton Street** where, at the corner of Draycott Avenue, there is an art gallery that specialises in eighteenth- and nineteenth-century dog portraits. The window was dominated by an oil painting of a Dobermann protecting her litter from a West Highland terrier. As we peered through the window, a couple in their forties approached walking a papillon that growled and charged at the door.

'He's touchy about them,' commented his mistress, pointing at the plaster statuettes of dogs in the window as she tugged him away from the shop.

'Christopher Plummer and Elaine Taylor lived here,' added Julia, and we quick marched down **Draycott Avenue** as the rain started again, turned right into **Bray Place** and immediately left on to **Anderson Street**.

Across the **King's Road** we entered **Royal Avenue**.

'Donovan lived here,' added Julia, who I hadn't realised was such a treasure trove of 1960s estate agent chatter.

**Burtons Court** ahead of us was horrifically wounded by the hurricane, with entire arcades of trees torn from the ground. As it can only be used by residents, who are recognised by the gate-keeper, we circled around it along **St Leonard's Terrace** and walked down **Ormonde Gate** towards the entrance to **The Royal Hospital**. Only dogs in residence at the hospital are allowed to use this entrance to the grounds so we walked from **Royal Hospital Road** down **Tite Street** to the **Chelsea Embankment**.

The Royal Hospital grounds and Ranelagh Gardens looked inviting to my canines but it was now raining even harder. We

95

walked along the Embankment, the dogs standing up to look over the wall down to the Thames where low tide revealed the litter of supermarket trolleys and the outfall of the Westbourne, the river that has its source back at Whitestone Pond at the heights of Hampstead.

Upon reaching Chelsea Bridge, I explained its Canadian connection to Julia: because so much British Columbian douglas fir was used in its construction, the Canadian Prime Minister was invited to open it. Julia rolled her eyes and we marched on, side-stepping the droppings left by countless Chelsea dogs on their way to Battersea Park.

An exhausted-looking Dobermann attached by a heavy chain to his tattooed male owner passed by us on the bridge but all of us, surprisingly even the dogs, had had enough for the day.

# Walk Six

## Battersea Park to
## Eel Brook Common

START: Chelsea Bridge entrance
to Battersea Park, SW11.

END: Eel Brook Common at
New King's Road, SW6.

LENGTH: Approximately 5 miles.

TIME: Approximately 2½ hours.

LEADS: No leads required but
in Battersea Park 'dogs must be
under your control'.

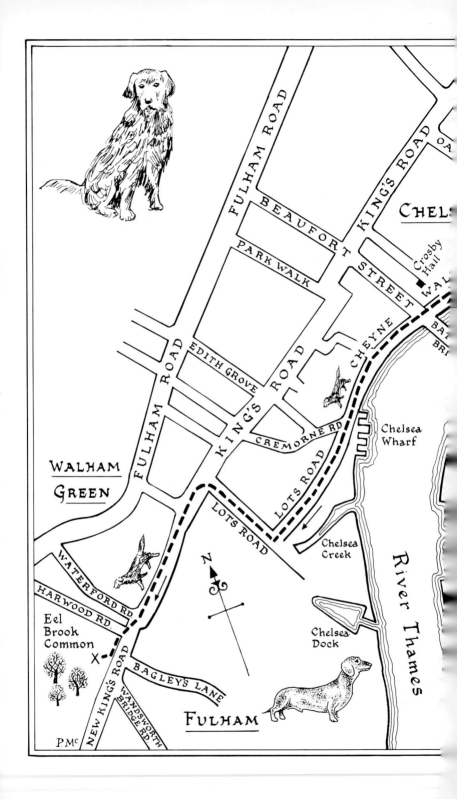

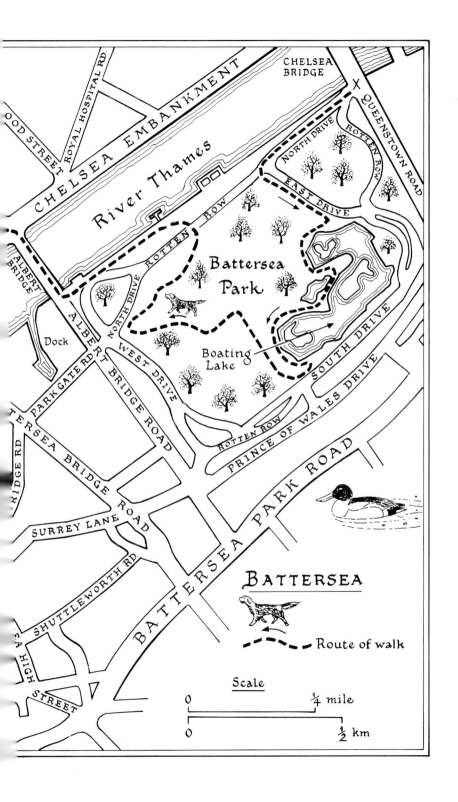

## From Battersea Park along the Chelsea Embankment to Eel Brook Common

The fog was dense over the Thames and the tide was rapidly coming in as we reached the Chelsea Bridge entrance to Battersea Park. It was a classic November day in London, Dickens weather, Conan Doyle weather. The total environment looked and felt like an old film set – and I rather enjoyed it.

I half expected to see Alec Guinness and the Lavender Hill mob dart out from the mist, but instead saw designer dogs. Every car in the parking lot by the embankment was either holding a dog, letting one out or awaiting one's return. The open tailgate of a Mercedes estate was welcoming back two Cavalier King Charles spaniels into a massive blanket-lined wicker basket. The dogs' owner, dressed in the uniform of a City businessman, was urging his charges to leap back into bed, something in fact, that Julia was quite keen to do.

A Porsche somehow disgorged a Weimaraner and an Irish setter leapt from the front curbside door of a taxi. Two Norwich terriers were vainly trying to jump back into their mistress's car, imploring her to help them while a boxer, all brakes on, was being dragged back to his Ford Sierra. This was an unexpected canine fashion parade. I thought I'd see only Battersea Dogs' Home dogs in Battersea Park.

We left the **North Drive** by the Thames and, armed with machetes to cut through the fog, walked along the **East Drive** towards the boating lake, passing four workmen sitting with military neatness on a fallen tree and drinking tea. Liberty and Lexington bounded Bambi-like into and out of the fog, graciously thanking us each time we came back in view for bringing them to such an exciting place. We passed the tennis courts to the left where, surprisingly, one court was being used, then past the garden for disabled people, a horticultural display especially set up for easy access if you are confined to a wheelchair. Lib tried to enter it but I told her I'd break her leg if she did and we continued our walk, passing a brown dog with a white leg and a white dog with a black leg, both on leads and both walked by elderly ladies. These were undoubtedly local dogs, quite distinct from the upwardly mobile beasts I had just seen in the car park.

On the plane-tree-lined arcade of **Central Drive** there was little storm damage – only fallen branches – and we walked on, skirting the lake, through verges of overgrown tall weeds turned rust-coloured by autumn frost, and up the slight hill that forms an isthmus between the boating lake and the foetid stagnant pond to its north. The sight of magpies surprised me. In my mind they are birds of the open countryside, startlingly black and white, a visual treat, but unpleasant in their behaviour with their taste for newly hatched blackbirds.

To our right, on the highest point of ground, was a statue of a dog and on its plinth a plaque which read, 'In memory of the brown terrier dog done to death in the laboratories of University College in February 1905. Men & Women of England. How long shall these things be?' There were paw prints on the plinth. Dog-walkers obviously stop and make their charges read these words. For me there was added interest as the sculptor was a woman named Nicola Hicks, a no-nonsense sparkly young lady whose bitch I had recently spayed.

The wording on this little monument is regrettably the work of a humaniac. 'Done to death.' Its plaintive call for dog-lovers of the world to unite and rise up against this canine oppression is, even more unfortunately, almost humorous and diminishes the serious-ness of the problem. A monument to a mouse or rat, the most common laboratory animals, would of course be equally unpro-ductive. The right mammal has been chosen, but it would be far more effective to place the problem in the present day. We are, today, almost a century after that dog's death, still using far more animals in research than we need to. Through tissue culture techniques and other new methods it would be possible, at a stroke, to halve the number of animals sacrificed in research. That isn't to say that animals should not be used in research. I have participated in a research project involving new-born piglets in which our object was to perfect a technique for saving human babies born with diaphragm holes or tears. I consider that a worthy enough cause. And in the context of our most urgent medical problem, an AIDS vaccine will not be developed without the ultimate use of cats and monkeys in the final stages of its development.

While I was thinking these thoughts, Julia had wandered on with the dogs around to the boating lake where she was viewing the Aylesbury ducks with a cook's eye. An Irish setter joined Lex as she swam out towards the island. The setter's owner, the cabbie from the car park, was not amused.

'She's in there like a shot if I don't stop 'er. She intentionally tries to lose me so that she can go for a swim. I don't know why I ever stop 'ere! Now, if she brought me one of those ducks it would be different, wouldn't it.'

The dog's master was dressed in a canary yellow wool jumper with Pringle none too discreetly inscribed upon it, grey flannel trousers and white patent leather slip-on shoes. His hair looked blow dried and he was carrying his large wallet. I asked him how often he comes here.

'My wife works now so there's no one home to take care of the dog. She's my dog an' all so I take 'er to work with me. If she needs to pee or lark about and I'm near a park I stop. I got towels to dry 'er and I keep a horse blanket in the boot for when she's wet. It stops 'er smell from bothering the fares.'

Julia placed an enforcement order on our dogs and they dutifully returned to her. We all turned back, away from the rowing boats moored at the far eastern end of the lake, and walked in a westerly direction. I mentioned to the cabbie that I had previously noticed that all cabbies take their wallets with them if they leave their cabs if only for a few seconds.

'There are villains everywhere, but this place is terrible. The car parks are the worst. There used to be two classes in Battersea, the working class and the criminal class. There are still two classes. Now it's the criminal class and the yuppies.'

He departed in the direction from which we had come and we continued along the lake. October's gale had felled some trees here, but the exotics – the Kentucky coffee tree, the maidenhair, the Chinese thuja – all remained. The most serious damage seems to have fallen upon the thirstiest trees, the oaks, planes and willows. From the fact that these oddities were still standing I assumed that they consumed little water, like holly and mulberry.

Battersea Park was London's second true purpose-created public park. (Victoria Park in the East End was the first.) The land on which we were now walking was originally marshland, flooded at high tide. A rough embankment was built hundreds of years ago to keep out the Thames, but it wasn't until the 1840s that the land was reclaimed. The earth we were walking on now was from the East End, hundreds of thousands of cubic yards of earth brought here when the Victoria Docks were being created. The argument for a park in this part of London was that it would distract the poor from the vices of the city – drinking, crime and prostitution – and help to bring the 'lower orders' in touch with their 'natural superiors'.

A feeble elderly man with a small and stiff old dog passed us and he doffed his cap. A couple, arm in arm, of equal vintage, followed behind walking their more spritely mutt. These were all undoubtedly original Battersea dogs and original Battersea dog-owners.

At the far end of the lake a young mother with her baby in a pram was feeding the swans while her cairn terrier tried to feed on the swans. The black swans she was feeding had been bred on Duck Island in St James's Park. I noticed that prams arrive here much earlier than they do on Hampstead Heath. Another pram passed, with a Yorkie in it. Julia and I stared at each other but were too embarrassed to ask the pram's serious-looking middle-aged female driver exactly what she was doing.

'Lexy, come on or the swans will get you,' urged Julia, and we rounded the lake.

Liberty eyed the masses of goose droppings but contented herself with rolling on the dead waterlogged leaves on the shore-line. As she was doing so, a skein of at least twenty Canada geese flew over her thunderously, landing only a short distance away on the water. Canada geese are migratory birds. In North America they fly thousands of miles each spring and autumn, but here in London, their instinctive urge to migrate takes them each day only from park to park. Somehow it saddens me to see them behave so.

As we walked towards **South Drive**, a muscle-bound jogger passed us, followed by a two-pound flying Yorkie.

'That little Yorkie running with that butch man. It looks so sweet,' said Julia.

I took off at speed and my dogs followed. 'How does this grab you?' I shouted from a distance, but she was talking to a young hound wearing a green fluorescent tag on its collar.

Upon my return she told me that he'd won it at a game of cards on Guy Fawkes night.

At South Drive we turned and walked back to the west of the lake. This area was once a sub-tropical garden with tree ferns, palms and giant grasses, but like most of Battersea Park has faded into a nondescript hodge-podge of water, trees, grass and shrubs.

There's no special or unique feel to the place as there is to the other green spaces we had walked through, no feeling of a master hand planning a total environment. The impression is that of an uneasy mélange of ideas with no co-ordinating theme. The consequence is that I felt I could be anywhere.

We walked past a magnificent conker tree where a policeman, a member of the Wandsworth Parks Police, was taking notes on a heavy broken branch that was caught in the tree. I asked him about dogs.

'We'd like dog-owners to use the area outside the ring road for dog-walking. We've got a baseball ground, an American football field and several football pitches and for some reason that's where dog-owners take their dogs to do their business. Lots of bull terriers now. Some kids are using them as offensive weapons. We had a robbery where a boy used his dog to corner a victim.'

I asked whether the Parks Police had their own dogs and he replied that they do. At least one is always in the park on duty. 'All German shepherds except for two schnauzers, but they're not so good. We use them to surprise flashers up on Mist's Pitch and to patrol the car parks and move on the undesirables who hang about in the men's toilets.'

Mist's Pitch is on the site of the old ash dump for the miniature railway at the north-east corner where we started our walk. This two acres of nature reserve is filled with nesting cover for birds and has at least seventeen different breeding butterflies.

'A bunch of orientals robbed a courting couple in the conservation area this summer but the dogs helped us get most of them. We had an act of piracy on the lake, too. Two young lads in their boat were ordered on to the island by some other lads who robbed them, took their clothes and their boat and left them.'

I checked my pockets, counted my feet and we moved on. Liberty and Lexington in the meantime had found a Rottweiler pup and were top and tailing it. The owner, a young man in his late teens or early twenties, looked concerned, so I called my dogs and offered an apology.

'That's OK. See this tear in me jacket? A Rottweiler did that trying to get me pup. I 'ad Jason up in me arms to protect 'im.'

I asked if it had happened here and he told me no, it was just outside the park, on Prince of Wales Drive. 'There's this man Tony with a Rottweiler that's always in mischief. 'E won't keep 'is dog on a lead and the dog saw Jason and ran straight across the road to get 'im. You should see the bruise 'e gave me. I've tried to make friends with Tony so 'e controls 'is dog when Jason's around, but 'e likes the brute the way 'e is. Funny, innit? Tony says 'e can tell when 'is dog's in a rage cause 'is eyes go black, but I can't see it.'

Funny but dangerous. That's a problem with Rottweilers and

with other potentially dangerous dogs. First of all, it's often the wrong people who keep them. And then, with the Rottweiler in particular, they don't give the danger signals that other dogs give – the low growl, hackles up, head lowered, ears flat, tail out. Their eyes dilate. That's all. What a threat signal!

Jason lolloped off under the watchful eye of his master while we walked back towards Central Drive observing several dogs to our left defecating on the playing fields exactly as the parks police had described. The fog was thinning but still thick enough to hide the tops of the trees or anything over a hundred yards away. Charging out of it came a massive male Dobermann.

'Dread! Come!' came a voice from the distance, and he didn't. But Dread did regain his manners and perfunctorily tried to sniff Liberty, who gave him her impression of a whirling dervish.

Lexington paced peripherally then joined in the olfactory happenings. I wish I could scent like a dog. The neurophysician Oliver Sacks in his book *The Man Who Mistook His Wife for a Hat* recounts the case of a young doctor who, upon awakening from a self-inflicted drug overdose with fashion drugs, found that his ability to smell things had been amazingly enhanced. He could recognise each of his twenty ward patients by their scent. His olfactory system was barraged with scent pictures. He could smell fear, contentment, sex. He could scent as a dog scents. This enhancement, this augmented scent ability, only lasted a short time and gradually faded but while his brain repaired from the damage caused by his drug abuse, he regained his lost sensitivity to smell, an ability that all of us have hidden in the primitive ancestral recesses of our brains.

Dread's owner appeared, and he was a classic case of an owner looking like his dog: black, in his late teens, he was wearing a shiny leather jacket.

Julia commented to him how handsome his dog was.

'He was a hard dog. I had to rescue him from a friend who couldn't handle him. It's taken two years to regain authority over him and make him safe but I still worry about him sometimes.'

I asked him if he knew the history of the breed and upon receiving a negative reply couldn't help but explain. 'Around a century ago there was a German tax collector, Herr Dobermann, who wanted a tough-looking dog to accompany him on his collecting rounds. Through crossing the Rottweiler with one of the local German hounds he created the dog that bears his name.'

Dread's owner liked that story. 'Hey, that's neat. It's been wonderful talking to you. Take care now.' And he and Dread were off.

Julia melted with his 'Take care'. No sooner had he left than Gracie, a bull terrier, arrived with Oscar, a springer spaniel pup, in her mouth. Libby liked this game and joined in. Everyone chases Oscar until he's caught. Oscar liked it most and the three dogs made figures of eight through the trees until Gracie's owner came on the scene, leashed her and dragged her away.

We crossed Central Drive and walked on towards the embankment and the **Peace Pagoda**, meeting Boy the 'bopping' West Highland terrier and his very anglicised American owner. 'Bopping' is one of Julia's words and describes a dog's action when he kicks up dirt with his hind feet either to mark his territory or cover his droppings. It's one of many words unique to her vocabulary. Lexington, for example, when groaning with pleasure 'wuffles'. A hound's-tooth suit on television goes 'jizzy'. The editor of the Oxford English Dictionary has said that the centre of evolution of the English language has left these shores and now resides in America, but he hasn't met my wife.

Boy bopped then approached Lib and tried to place his head on her back.

'He has to do that to prove he's a man,' explained his owner.

He tried it on Lib and she rolled over.

There were pigeons everywhere here, wood pigeons and feral pigeons. Feral pigeons are real home bodies. They're as parochial as most native Londoners and seldom leave the precincts in which they were born and raised. These were Battersea pigeons and always would be Battersea pigeons. The tree damage along the embankment on both sides of the Peace Pagoda was severe, with many fallen planes already carved into massively pruned trunks and logs. The dogs rolled in the accumulated mulch of sawdust then both of them suddenly sat bolt upright and raced to the retaining wall of the embankment. They stood up on their hind legs 'wuffling' as they caught scent of the Thames below.

The scene on the river reminded me of Venice in the winter, the colours and sounds muted by the fog. Barges silently glided past each other while on the far side traffic was at an eerie standstill. Only the ghostly images of trees in the south grounds of the Royal Hospital and Ranelagh Gardens were visible. The spires of Chelsea Bridge were lost in the mist. King Charles II used to swim in the river, here in front of the Royal Hospital, and it was from where we were now standing that Colonel Blood hid in the rushes in his attempt to assassinate the king.

This embankment was the first to be built, in 1860. The Chelsea Embankment opposite was completed in 1871. The combination of the two meant that there would never again be a frost fair on the frozen Thames: the current now is too strong for ice to form. Also, the tide comes much further up the river now.

As we turned left towards Albert Bridge, a free-range dog, a black and white terrier, appeared at my side, sat and begged. There wasn't an owner in sight. He didn't look undernourished, but he followed us, mournful eyes pleading with us.

Julia has an uncanny ability to find stray dogs – a springer spaniel once appeared from nowhere and hopped in her car on an empty country road in the back of beyond in Ontario – so I explained to her that this was a professional begging dog. London has a history of them. Boer War veterans had a brigade of them organised to raise money for the wounded. One called Tim sat outside Paddington Station raising money for widows of railway workers, while London Jack fulfilled the same function outside Waterloo Station. Tramps still use them today throughout central London. This was simply a begging dog, I told her, that had lost its begging cup. She didn't believe me. Fortunately the little beggar's owner appeared and he ran off.

Walking westwards we passed several plane trees that had fallen over the embankment and crashed down into the Thames below. One-inch-thick ropes tied them to the retaining wall, preventing them from drifting dangerously into deeper waters. The dogs continued to leap up at the wall, desperate to get nearer the water. 'They'd be idiot enough to jump in,' I thought, and commanded them away from the wall.

The tide was still tearing its way up river and that combined with the run-off from recent rain had created a massive turbulence under the surface. Julia told me she'd jump in to save them if Lib or Lex fell in and I reminded her that she can swim as well as our parrot. Deep down I knew that my instinctive reaction would be the same. You live with another sentient living creature long enough and it becomes more than an animal. It becomes a personality with whom you share your home and for whom you feel a responsibility. I hope that I would have the common sense *not* to jump into the Thames if my dog fell in, but fear that the emotional would overwhelm the rational.

A dachshund snaked past us in the opposite direction as we turned away from the embankment, across **Rotten Row** and along **North Drive** towards the herb garden, tucked away in an old courtyard. The courtyard itself looked like a tip, but the herbs made up as comprehensive a collection as I'd ever seen. The dogs were leashed at the 'dog park' while Julia and I reconnoitred. There were fifty-four different varieties of thyme alone.

Having been left on their own for ten minutes, the dogs were overjoyed at their leaders' return and smothered us with affection. We walked back on West Drive to the embankment and then out of the park where there was a sign on the railings stating that within the park 'Dogs must be kept under control', a more sensible and realistic regulation than 'Dogs must be kept on leads' as in theory a lead isn't always necessary to control a dog.

All troops must break step on **Albert Bridge** when marching across and we instructed the dogs to obey. As we crossed, a massive barge passed directly beneath us. I was amazed at the speed with which it moved and the minimal clearance it had. The noise was oppressive on the other side. Traffic was no longer at a standstill.

A strip of greenery separates **Cheyne Walk** from the juggernauts on Chelsea Embankment and we walked along this, with the dogs kept on their leads, meeting a corgi in front of **Thomas Carlyle's statue**. I asked Julia if she had ever read Carlyle, but she couldn't hear me. The traffic noise was overwhelming. Local noise bothered Carlyle, too, but it was different back in the 1800s. His wife Jane wrote diplomatic letters to owners of cocks, parrots, macaws and barking dogs asking them to keep their livestock silent – but to little avail. Carlyle also had a love-hate relationship with his wife's dog Nero. He would take Nero with him on his long nightly walks and referred to the dog in his writing as 'the vermin' and 'the miserable quadruped', but when Nero was run over by a butcher's cart and died Carlyle wrote that his heart was 'unexpectedly and distractedly torn to pieces'. His wife Jane, on the other hand, was made of stiffer stuff. Attitudes to life and especially animal life were different in the 1800s, but on one occasion after an unknown incident the usually tender-hearted Jane ordered one of her cats to be drowned in the Thames for 'unexampled' dishonesty! The drowning was executed where we were now standing at the foot of **Church Street**, opposite a waterfront pub called The Dog, that then stood there.

A feral pigeon was sitting on Thomas More's head as we passed his statue – a fitting composition. Animals were obviously important to More as Holbein's portrait of the More family, in nearby Crosby Hall, includes the dog, and Erasmus wrote that, 'All the birds in Chelsea come to him to be fed.' As a tingle of light, the faintest of pink, broke through the fog giving even the massive transport trucks a gentle reflective glow, it became clear to me why so many of Britain's renowned painters chose to have their studios on Cheyne Walk. Turner, Whistler, Rossetti – all lived and painted here. Dante Gabriel Rossetti was by far the most animal mad. He kept two kangaroos, but one killed the other then his racoon finished off the survivor. His armadillos once burrowed under his walls and turned up in his neighbour's kitchen. The famous and the familiar still choose Cheyne Walk as their home: Keith Richard, Mick Jagger, Jane Asher and Gerald Scarfe have all lived in these houses.

There is a small sunken garden just past Church Street that we nipped into and out of, then we crossed **Beaufort Street** at Battersea Bridge and returned to the river side of Cheyne Walk, past the agglomeration of houseboats. A river dog, a rust-coloured twenty-pound mongrel with a heavy fur ruff, stood barking at us from his barge and it intrigued Liberty and Lexington that such noises could come from the river. They eyed the green grass of a small park, **Cremorne Gardens**, jutting out into the Thames, but it was signposted that no dogs were allowed so we marched on.

The original Cremorne Gardens were far larger, spreading from the nearby King's Road down to the river. As ballooning had been fashionable in Green Park, so it became here. On one occasion, a Mme Poitevin, dressed only in a scarlet tunic and a wreath of roses, ascended sidesaddle on a violently kicking bull to return to earth five hours later in Ilford, Essex. Sometimes ascents were made on horseback. A veterinary surgeon appealed against the 'sport' saying that the animals were subjected to appalling discomfort, fear and pain, but it was not until one of the animals wrote a letter to *The Times* that the entertainment was stopped. A letter to the Editor from 'The Bull in the Balloon' described the suffering and humiliation that he endured on these flights and in 1852 they finally ceased.

Cheyne Walk, the most sought-after of riverfront accommodation, became **Lots Road**, once described as the most desolating street in all of London. The power station here used to provide electricity for the entire Underground system, and even today the humming noise from its generators permeates the area. We marched the dogs on, past a stripped pine shop and a freshly minted development of showrooms, one of which contained displays of kitchen units. Julia gave me the leads of both still muddy and wet dogs and went in to look at the limed cupboards. As I stood outside whistling sweet nothings, the manager of the shop came to the door.

'Oh, do come in. The floors are wood. I can show you where my dog used to sleep.' She looked up at me. 'You can come in, too.'

Another anglicised American, and, lo and behold, her dog basket was still in situ.

Julia came out beaming, having picked up ideas for painting, panelling and curtain-making.

Where Lots Road turns sharp right towards the King's Road it is lined with auction houses. Fortunately, no auctions were in progress and, followed by a large black latchkey dog, we marched on to **Westfield Gardens** where the dogs were released from their bonds.

This is a new green space, created by tearing down derelict terraced houses and blocking off several streets. It was a pleasant and unexpected venue for Julia and me and also for the dogs who, still followed by the latchkey dog, ran up to Rosie, an eighteen-month-old Staffordshire bull terrier and asked her to dance. Which she did.

As the sun broke through the haze, the dogs danced, arm-wrestled and played tag, all the time with the free-range dog attached to their behinds. I'd been surprised at how few uncontrolled dogs we had encountered on our walk so far, but then again we'd been walking through some pretty smart territory. We'd also been walking through the most dogless part of London.

There are half as many dogs in this part of London, the north-west, as there are, for example, in the south-east of the metropolitan area. To let a dog wander freely in London, an owner must either have a misguided belief that dogs should be as free as the birds, independent of human constraints, free to live by their wits in a Thoreau-like wilderness, or be too senseless and moronic to understand the dangers involved. I find the former more annoying because it's the behaviour of the otherwise intelligent and educated owners who have dogs for the wrong reasons. The stray dog problem is of course not what it once was. At the turn of the century, the cat-meat man, who delivered horsemeat on skewers to cat-owners, putting it through letterboxes in their absence, was followed by hordes of dogs. It's only on some council estates that you still find packs of latchkey dogs today.

Westfield Gardens is well planned. There is a large dog-free children's area and a large dog area. Even the sign, 'Please train your dog to use the area provided and not foul the remainder of the park', reeks of common sense.

At **King's Road** we turned left and walked the bridge over the railway and Chelsea Creek, one of the lost rivers of London. This one, rising as Counter's Creek in Kensal Green cemetery, is responsible for countless damp buildings from Shepherd's Bush to Earl's Court. The section we were walking over was once a canal a hundred feet wide but it failed commercially and the space was bought by the railway.

Julia paused at an antique shop and closely studied the painted furniture. Across the road, a moustached Irishman wearing a three-piece bell-bottomed navy blue striped suit and platform shoes was wheeling a chest of drawers from one antique shop to the next. He held doorstep conversations with the shop owners and their ever-present dogs in the now brilliant sunshine trying his luckless sales pitch. We crossed over to a pine shop on the north side, guarded by a somnolent old English sheepdog, and went in. While the owner was warning us of the unpredictable nature of her dog, he followed Lex and Lib in and gave them a peremptory sniff. I explained that I was a vet, a fairly pointless observation in the circumstances, but one that seems to calm people when they are dog worried and while Julia examined the paint jobs I talked dogs with the owner, a tall streaked blonde from the sixties.

'I took him to my vet, who I've known for years, because of the dog's rheumatism, and while I was there I mentioned that the torn cartilages in my knee were acting up again so he told me to put my leg up on the table. He touched my knee and sure enough it felt better for three days!'

I knew her vet, a handsome devil, someone who looks a bit like a rugger-playing leprechaun, and asked her if she went back often.

'Oh yes. He's a conventional vet but he also practises touch-healing. An Irish lady was there with her dog. It had a tumour on its head but she was going back to Ireland for a holiday and wouldn't be able to come in for surgery until the end of the summer, so the vet told her to touch-heal it in the meantime. Six months of faith-healing and the tumour was gone.'

Julia came over to ask about the furniture and I excused myself to look at a table and chairs in the basement, taking Lexington with me. While I was looking at the paintwork, Lex suddenly barked and cowered. Under a sideboard there was a red and white teddy bear which she was certain was going to attack and devour her. I commanded her to sit, which she did with a shiver, and picked up the teddy bear. She pulled back, but I stroked the toy and sniffed it and she relaxed a little until finally she was willing to smell it too. I then let her eat it, which she did with glee, before placing it back on its shelf and returning upstairs.

Outside, we passed three small black mongrels being walked by two men and continued west. Frank Manolson, the only other Canadian vet who has practised in London, set up the veterinary surgery to our left. A unique man, he both drank and wrote prolifically and was excruciatingly funny and ribald until his premature death.

Around the bend on **New King's Road** was **Eel Brook Common**, the end of our walk. It was now a gloriously sunny day and I contemplated continuing on to Putney Bridge, but decided against it. The dogs were let off their leads and raced ahead while we sauntered to a bench facing the sun and sat down. Sitting on a parallel bench was a man in his forties with a white cane. As Liberty approached to sniff his knees I called her to come. He must have smelt good, for she disobeyed and as he felt her breath on his leg he smiled and reached forward with a downturned hand. Liberty licked his hand and as he tickled her neck I walked over and sat down, apologising for my dog's behaviour. Lib had found a friend and by now had buried her head between his knees and was on the receiving end of a two-handed head rub.

'She's a golden, isn't she? She's got the head of a bitch. I lost mine recently.'

I asked if his had been a working guide dog and he said that she had.

'I had her for eight years. She was part of me. She gave me freedom. Before I lost my sight I was quite active – football, tennis, skiing. I didn't see how I could manage without my sight.' He continued to stroke Libby, to caress her. 'A few weeks ago she started leaving some of her meal. She still worked well and enjoyed her exercise, but I took her to my vet who diagnosed fluid in her abdomen. He took a sample of the fluid and a blood sample. The results which came back showed that she might have a serious problem but by then she was really slowing down. Never wanted to stop working though. Throughout it all, she still wanted to work for me. She worked right up to her last trip to the vet's. She walked me there. He rang me an hour later with the bad news. She had liver cancer and it had spread everywhere, so there was nothing to do but put her down. We've always come here, each day, so that Princess could have a run off her lead.'

The blind man was rocking ever so gently as he spoke and his fingers buried themselves deeper in Libby's fur. 'She died last week, but I can't stop coming here. Not yet. I'll be getting another dog in a few months and I know she'll be a good worker, but it will never be like Princess. She was something extra special. You can't describe it in words. She gave her life for me and gave me something I never thought I'd have again. She gave me back my self-esteem. She gave me back my dignity.'

Sadness is an inevitable part of owning a dog, if only because their lives are so short and the grief we feel is so intense, in many ways the same as the grief we feel when human companions die. The loss that this dignified man had suffered was even more cruel because of the unique relationship that develops between a blind person and his guide dog, a relationship of mutual interdependence. But I also knew that, with time, his pain would change to reminiscence and ultimately to memories of the joys he had had with his dog. That is what happens with most dog-owners. Over seventy-five per cent of us bring new dogs into our homes within a year of the death of our previous ones, as positive a signal as there can be of the joys of canine companionship.

# *Walk Seven*

## Eel Brook Common to Putney Embankment

**START:** Eel Brook Common at New King's Road, SW6.

**END:** The Embankment, Putney, SW15.

**LENGTH:** Approximately 4 miles.

**TIME:** Approximately 2½ hours.

**LEADS:** Dogs are not allowed on football pitches in South Park, must be on leads in Hurlingham Gardens and 'under your control' in Bishop's Park. Dogs are not allowed in the Moat Gardens or the grounds of Fulham Palace.

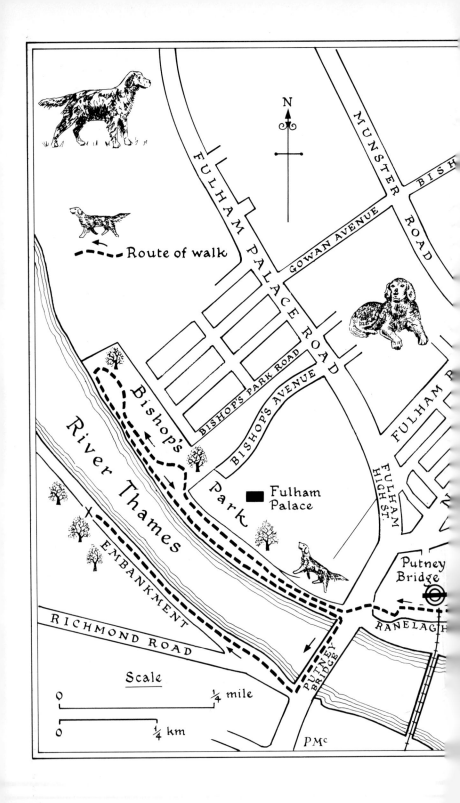

N

Route of walk

FULHAM PALACE ROAD

GOWAN AVENUE

MUNSTER ROAD

BISH

River Thames

Bishop's Park

BISHOPS PARK ROAD

BISHOPS AVENUE

Fulham Palace

FULHAM P

FULHAM HIGH ST.

EMBANKMENT

Putney Bridge

RICHMOND ROAD

RANELAGH

PUTNEY BRIDGE

Scale

0                          ¼ mile

0                          ¼ km

PMᶜ

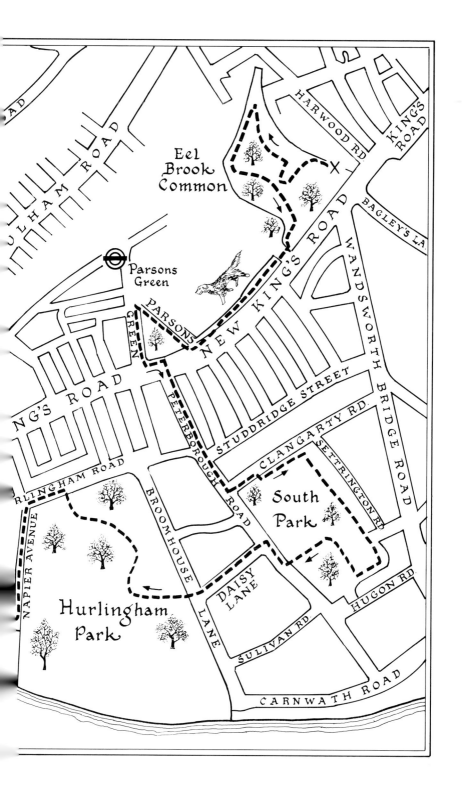

## From Eel Brook Common via Hurlingham Park and Bishop's Park to Putney Embankment

Eel Brook Common is but a remnant of a once larger common, whittled away over the centuries by its hereditary landowners. The last strip of common that was lost before public rights were enshrined in law went to the District Line of the Underground, which here, of course, is overground. It leaves a narrow strip which like a withered finger leads from the body of the park up towards the Fulham Broadway Underground station. Eel Brook Common is small, but large enough, still, to exercise a dog.

It was another opalescent November morning, cold and explosively windy – portents that the weather could either dramatically improve or deteriorate – as Julia, Liberty, Lexington and I ventured on to this flat and faceless space. Originally called Hillbrook Common, any vestige of a local hill here disappeared centuries ago. It was as flat and as featureless as is all of Fulham.

The dogs performed their usual early morning antics, ritually racing about smelling the scent trails of earlier visitors. They enjoyed the wind up their tails but Julia found it less to her liking, walking backwards into the wind as we made a figure of eight on this twenty-acre patch of green. Three latchkey dogs worked the perimeter of the common near the train line, sniffing and marking as we watched a German shepherd and a beagle obediently leave with their owners. Everyone was bundled in winter coats and heavy woollen scarves. All would undoubtedly have far preferred to be in their own warm homes but for the obligation to give their dogs their early-morning exercise.

A Jack Russell terrier bounded up to Liberty, tripping over her own muscles as she did so, and asked Lib if she'd like to chase her. This intrigued Lexington, who during our walks has become a much more self-confident dog, and she arrived to investigate what was being planned.

'Be careful of Posy,' her owner hoarsely called down from the path. 'She's a little thug.'

Ambling along beside Posy's owner were two mature clumber spaniels. Each spaniel was working his own side of the path, seemingly vacuuming the grass with its nose. Their owner's nose was her prominent feature, too, cherry red from either the wind or a nasty cold.

Her clumbers, Humphrey and Brompton, were peripatetic dogs, I discovered, having lived in New York and Hong Kong before settling in Fulham. The word Fulham jarred somehow after Hong Kong and New York. Chelsea or Hampstead would sound more apposite. Even Bloomsbury would suggest an iconoclastic preference for the elegant but unusual. Fulham, on the other hand, suggests jumped-up estate agents and commodity traders in matt black turbo-charged cars with go-faster stripes painted on the wings. Its men in red prison-bar striped shirts and the women with rouched curtains in every window of their homes, all speaking in slightly too perfect tones and accents. This, on the other hand, was a classy lady, even with a red nose.

'The dogs love it here and it's only a minute from their house to the common. That's why I moved. They're both getting on now and can't take too much exercise. In fact, I was so worried about Humphrey last spring that I took him to the vet to discuss you know what.'

Humphrey was doddering near by and didn't know what 'you know what' meant.

'He was getting very weak on his pins, but he seemed to know why I had taken him there. The vet gave him an injection and some pills and he positively floated out of the surgery. It was amazing. Do you know what my vet said? When I told him that I thought Humphrey knew why I was there, he said, "Absolutely. Whenever my old dog looks creaky I just get out the old shotgun and stand it up against the wall. That instantly perks him up."'

Posy was now back with her clumbers, having run my dogs into the ground, and was licking the discharge from Brompton's eyes.

Her owner was dying from the cold and started making down the path towards the New King's Road, calling for her pack to follow her.

'I wish my ex had taken them this morning,' she said. 'He comes around for breakfast each morning to see the children and play with the dogs but still leaves it to me to give them their exercise.'

As in Hampstead, the wives always get custody of the dogs. I only know of one contrary instance, a client of mine who divorced his wife but continued to live in their matrimonial home for another year because he wanted the dog and his wife wouldn't part with it. Just when the problem was reaching critical mass, the ex-wife found another fellow and lost her interest in the mutt.

The classy lady backed out of the common and we walked on.

119

'What a nice tail,' Julia remarked.

It's fascinating how the meanings of expressions change with time. Julia's comment was a daily suggestion in the corridors of my high school and even at university, but now she was referring to a passing black mutt with a tail as feathery as an unpruned weeping willow.

'Tails are a real litmus paper of a dog's feelings and emotions,' she continued.

From the stance of this dog's tail as he sniffed Lexington, he was feeling and emotioning sex.

Eel Brook Common was well on its way to recovery from the gale. The trunks of the fallen plane trees were stripped and prepared for removal while branches and leaves had been mulched into tall mounds of sawdust and shavings. A Hammersmith and Fulham vacuum vehicle was religiously cleaning the grass on the western side of the park, making it putting-green clean. We walked with the dogs up to the northern perimeter, where there were tall grass and weeds growing by the chain-link fence. Liberty enjoyed a salad as she usually does after a little exercise and Lex joined in on the feast of couch grass and late-season sow thistle.

Many dog-owners think that their pets only eat grass to make themselves sick – the herbalist Thomas Culpeper certainly thought so – but it is often the case that dogs will eat greens like couch grass *after* they're sick, or simply because they like salads. Grasses are a rich source of minerals, carbohydrates and sugars.

Sow thistle is a fascinating weed. I'm sure that the herbal vet mentioned by the owner of the poor-visioned dog on Primrose Hill grows his own, for this is used as an age-old treatment for fevers and circulation disorders in domestic animals. According to Pliny, Theseus dined off a dish of sow thistle before capturing the rampaging bull on the plain of Marathon and presenting it to the goddess Athene. Pliny also thought it an excellent treatment for bad breath, so we let both dogs indulge to their hearts' content. When they had finished, Libby rolled on a mound of dry spongy branch mulch and Julia said that she wished she could do the same.

Yorkies and Cavalier King Charles spaniels criss-crossed the common tethered to their female owners, all on short snappy outings. One criss-cross of the park was enough for us, so we made our way back towards the main road followed closely by an English setter and then its owner in hot pursuit.

'Teaspoon's deaf,' she explained as she grabbed his collar, turned his head back towards the centre of the common and gave him a shove.

A narrow strip of fenced-off grass, a vestige of the former common land, runs along the north side of **New King's Road** and we followed the pavement outside it. One fenced section is for dog exercise and was being dutifully used by a German shepherd whose owner walked along outside the fence, no doubt to keep his shoes tidy. Another section is restricted to people and has benches on which one can sit and watch the traffic go by. Between the wars crowds used to gather on this narrow strip to watch Indian princes march their polo ponies to Hurlingham, a park we would be visiting later in the morning.

Attached to their leads, the dogs marched past the shops. You could tell the financial climate of the area by the products for sale: Australian blueberries at £4.00 for eight ounces. All of this flat and passionless landscape was, until the mid-nineteenth century, the market garden for London. Fruit and vegetables were grown here on rich alluvial river soil. Now only the vaguest of traces of that function remain, replaced by the now much sought-after and very fashionable yet repressively uniform row houses on their flat straight symmetrical streets. I must admit I find little to appreciate in Victorian architecture although I live in a Victorian house myself.

We entered **Parsons Green**, a postage stamp of trees and grass that was once common waste land of the old manor of Fulham, and the dogs were released from their oppressive leads. Here too the parks department was efficiently repairing the land from the ravages of the storm. Julia leapt up on to a mulch mound and bounced on it playing I'm the King of the Castle while I looked for the dogs who had disappeared behind fallen trees at the northern corner of the green.

Suddenly a flock of pigeons took to the air and a springer spaniel on roller skates appeared, closely followed by my dogs. The springer had a hollowed-out whole loaf of bread in her mouth which hid her face up to her eyes. She had obviously just stolen it from the pigeons, and my dogs wanted it! As hard and as fast as they chased her, the springer kept inches ahead. She zigged. She zagged. She leapt over branches, did U-turns, but small as she was she outmanoeuvred my retrievers. Her owner, a young woman hobbling in oversized slippers, was delighted.

'This is just what Lottie needs. I've got stitches in both feet and can't exercise her. I'm ever so grateful.'

By now Lottie, no more than nine months old, was being run into the ground by my more athletic twosome. They had the energy to maintain the chase, and the instinct and desire to do so, but Lottie was wilting. With a last burst of speed she distanced herself from her pursuers then spun on a sixpence, stopped, dropped her treasure and growled at her startled protagonists. Lib and Lex were perplexed. After all, it was only a game. I called them to me and they broke off.

A man in broken shoes with a rolled cigarette dangling from his lower lip was throwing a ball for Sheila, his four-year-old black and tan terrier, while his older and fatter black and tan sat on her butt staring into space.

'Nice dog you've got,' I said.

'Not mine,' he replied.

Julia and I put leads back on the dogs and crossed New King's Road, walking past the elegant row of Georgian houses that faces the south side of the green and turned right on to **Peterborough Road** leading to **South Park**.

South Park is the only large vestige of the original market gardens of Fulham. A frail elderly lady with a cane was leaving the grounds with her English bull terrier, an unlikely combination, as we entered the north gate by the football pitches. It was filled with black dogs, a black Shih Tzu with a man in green wellies, red trousers and a Barbour jacket, a black German shepherd, a black standard poodle playing tennis with his master, and two black mutts.

Along the eastern length of the park there is a fenced-off dog exercise area in which a massive Weimaraner was sniffing. His master walked along the path outside the exercise compound, swinging a chain lead that looked heavy enough to anchor the QE2. As Eel Brook Common was this morning a women's dog-walking area, South Park was today very much for the men. I wondered why they weren't working, something I've wondered throughout our walk as the number of male dog-walkers on each section of the journey has almost equalled that of females. Weekday male dog-walkers are a conundrum. Are they unemployed? Not, in most cases, if their clothes are anything to go by. Are they 'house-husbands' with working wives? Surely there can't be *that* many. I can only conclude that there are many men in London who have jobs that give them freedom to walk their dogs during the morning.

The air was no longer damp although the wind was still fierce as we walked south along the eastern perimeter of the park. In front of us were two corpulent dogs, a beagle and a corgi cross, both limping with what appeared to my professional eye to be ruptured cruciate ligaments.

'It makes me cross!' muttered the chief. 'It's really stupid!'

The black poodle, upon eyeing Lib and Lex, spat out his tennis ball and rambled over to them. He was a sorry mess, looking more like a moth-eaten wool coat than a dog. His skin was wrinkled and black, covered with thin straggly weedy hair. He had a visible fold of skin over the base of his tail and was probably about nine years old. He stank.

'Looks like an allergy to fleas,' I mentioned to his owner, a man in his early thirties in jeans, black Wellingtons and a Wimpy jacket.

'Can't get rid of them. Had the rodent man in and he couldn't get rid of them either. It's the cats that bring them in. I've got four cats and they give the fleas to the dog.'

I mulled over in my mind whether I should become involved in this one. It's always possible to get rid of fleas if you're willing to work at it. I looked at the dog, which I found out was in fact seven years old, and decided it was worth it. Starting with the 'I'm a vet and that dog of mine over there is allergic' routine, I explained how he must first deflea the cats and provide them with flea collars to prevent further infestations, then deflea the house and finally deflea the dog. November was the best time of year to do it for there would be a hard frost any time now which would eliminate outdoor fleas until the following summer.

Obligations over, Julia and I walked up to the small outdoor aviary in front of the central greenhouse, observed the birds, observed a border terrier trying to empty his anal glands by dragging his butt on the grass, then, following a black poodle in a red coat and a geriatric retriever bitch we left South Park by the western gate, crossed **Peterborough Road** and walked down the pollarded plane-tree-lined **Daisy Lane**. Somehow this beautifully maintained avenue fully escaped the depredations of the October storm. It was good to see.

The high brick wall of the Hurlingham Club stood before us but by turning right up **Broomhouse Lane** we came to an entrance to **Hurlingham Park**, that part of the Hurlingham Club which was compulsorily purchased about thirty-five years ago and is now

123

open to itinerant canines and their owners. On the flat open land that had once been the club's number one polo ground, trodden by the Indian princes' immaculate ponies, a golden retriever called Oscar was eating a piece of plastic while a giant of a collie peed on the football goalpost.

This was a fun stop for Liberty. There was a massive puddle, a lake really, between the football goalposts into which she launched herself. She wallowed like a water buffalo barking with delight. A little boy, certainly no more than two and a half, upon seeing the joy she was having joined her, jumping, splashing and shrieking with joy. Julia was concerned that Liberty would treat the little boy as a fellow canine and called her to 'come', which she obediently did, but as soon as she was off her 'call' she was back in, spinning like a top, bowing with her forepaws, then turning tight circles in the brown mire. Her human companion instantly rejoined her, sitting in the goo up to his waist. His mother was not amused.

Lexington contented herself with walking in black slime, painting her feet to look as if she was wearing rubber boots, then prancing off to investigate a passing Dobermann. Prince, another golden retriever, floated on to the scene and imperiously sniffed every-thing sniffable. He tried me, but I declined his advances. An Irish setter perambulated along and joined the gang, now a hard knot of big dogs but for a Scottish terrier in a tartan winter coat. The Scottie meticulously avoided walking on any damp spots as he took advantage of the play that was going on to have a good smell of the other dogs' behinds.

'Robbie's a canny Scot,' commented his equally tartan-lined owner. 'He knows the water is chilly and avoids it.'

It was Robbie's owner who told us the names of the other dogs.

'Look!' cried Julia. 'Prince is after my princess,' as we watched Prince come to the erroneous conclusion that Lexington was in season. Robbie in the meantime was lusting hopelessly after everything, finally contenting himself with the goalpost, the only object that failed to avoid his grasp.

We tiptoed through the mire, with the more densely tree-covered grounds of the still private Hurlingham Club to our left and proceeded northerly towards **Hurlingham Road**, where there is, in fact, an enclosed dog-walking area that no one was using until Oscar saw a squirrel and sailed sylph-like over the high fence in hot pursuit. Turning left on Hurlingham Road we passed Lord Beaverbrook's old home, The Vineyard, perhaps the largest private garden still extant in Fulham, and turned left again on to **Napier Avenue**.

There was little traffic, so I allowed the dogs to walk without their leads until we got to **Ranelagh Gardens** where we turned right and, with leads reapplied, passed under the railway bridge. If I didn't have the dogs with me I would have taken Julia into the River Café, an old tiled café in the classic English tradition, but contented myself with holding both leads as Julia peered through the windows. The gourmet shop next door told us that this was no longer the working-class area it was only a few years ago. In the window of Ranelagh Antiques were books such as *Hoof & Claw* and *The Days of Bruce*, but we walked on leaving two Westies to do the window-shopping. All of this area was once the site of the original Ranelagh Club before it moved across the river to what is now Barn Elms Park, just beyond the Putney Embankment.

Turning hard left it is possible to walk around a detritus-filled ditch laden with high-tide bits of Thames styrofoam down to the river itself. As we did so, the high winds blew away the last vestiges of clouds and we were suddenly bathed in trenchant sunshine. The contrast was swift and glorious.

In the river, by the mouth of the ditch, a heron was standing motionless as if mesmerised by the instantaneous brilliance of the light. It looked odd to see this elegant fisher here even though it was low tide, as I would have thought that all it would find in this hopelessly rubbish-filled patch would be old motorcycle chains. We surmised that it was a Regent's Park heron, off on a day's fishing.

Herons are early nesters in England and this one would soon be staking out its territory. The male sets up home then calls for a mate, an idea that Julia found rather comforting. As we watched our Thames heron, it took off from the shallows and with his neck fully extended flew a low wide circle out over the Thames towards Wandsworth Park on the far side then back towards us, whereupon he lowered his undercarriage until he was almost bolt upright, raised his black feathered wing flaps and landed deftly like a Harrier jet. We broke into applause, but were too far away for him to hear. Now we retraced our steps past the graffiti-laden hoardings and signs through the even more graffiti-lined underpass into the grounds of **Bishop's Park**, the ancient hunting land of the Bishop of London.

The manor of Fulham was granted to the Bishop of London in

the early eighth century. There must have been some buildings here at the time, because Vikings invaded Fulham in 879. However, it was probably as stimulating and as exciting then as it is now, for the dreaded invaders left almost immediately. With our dogs still on their leads, we turned towards the river, walking through the small ornamental garden. A giant swath of climbing ivy had been wrenched from the wall of the bridge in the storm and thrown down on the path with its sisal-like back exposed. The ivy flowers were in full bloom providing the only honey for insects from now until the spring. Its black berries would be ripe by Christmas, but neither Julia nor I could see how this giant drape of wall-covering could be rehung.

The embankment was built twenty-odd years after the Chelsea Embankment in the 1890s. We walked a short distance along it before releasing the dogs and walking back, away from the river, in the direction of Fulham Palace itself and up the steps of a small rock garden. The storm damage here in Bishop's Park was the worst we had yet seen. The borders of mature plane trees that run the length of the park had been ravaged. I counted thirteen trees down just in the space directly in front of us.

Here, too, there is a designated dog exercise area but its iron fencing had been utterly destroyed by falling trees. Liberty and Lexington dived through the leaves, removing as they did so some of their Hurlingham mud, while Julia and I viewed the sad panorama before us. I could see that the magnificent old cedar of Lebanon in the grounds of Fulham Palace was still dignified and upright and wondered about the other historic trees on the grounds. There are 'dog-free zones' here. The Warren Allotment Gardens, the Moat Gardens and Fulham Palace itself are all dog-free, so I wouldn't be able to find out today what else was destroyed. A number of Bishops of London over hundreds of years have been avid gardeners. The first tamarisk tree in Britain was planted here, as was the first magnolia. From the damage before us it appeared that a lot more planting would take place in the next few years.

The brilliant sunshine had drawn dogs and their owners from their nearby homes and Bishop's Park was packed with them. Four whippets, one of which was in a bulky winter coat that looked as if it weighed more than she did, and a Labrador were racing down the central avenue of the park. A man and a teenage boy were with them. The Labrador was released by the boy first and then, when it had run half the distance to the man, the whippets were unleashed.

'She thinks she's a whippet,' the owner explained as we walked past, 'so we treat her like one but give her a handicap.'

Over on the path by the embankment, a gloriously long-haired German shepherd was being dragged by his owner by the stick in his mouth. Bicyclists had appeared and Benjamin, a cocker spaniel, was doing his best to unmount them. There were two fires of branches of fallen trees burning in the middle of the central avenue and near by a four-wheel-drive pick-up truck was winching a massive branch, itself the size of a mature tree, towards a large pile of heavy and already cut branches. A black dog lay near one fire perusing the canine activity while his tree-surgeon master continued his work.

Beyond the fires, a tall, attractive, chestnut-haired girl was throwing a stick for her young golden retriever pup. I casually walked over, wondering whether her hair was really such a deliciously rich and luscious colour or whether it came out of a bottle, deciding before I got there that it really didn't matter. As I said hello, a matt black mongrel bitch hobbled into view barking furiously. She had a large cast on her left front leg but this wasn't going to deter her from protecting her mistress. A sheepdog sort of dog dithered in the background, her third charge. This was a very doggy lady.

Lexington came over too, showing no interest in the barker but keen to examine a retriever younger than herself. I commented to the dark-haired and very blue-eyed owner that she had a lot of dogs.

'I never planned to. Lucy (the sheepdog type) belonged to a boyfriend who left both of us. Busybody (with the cast) was a stray who I found in my kitchen two years ago and Flax (the retriever) just sort of happened.'

Things always 'just sort of happen' but only like this if you're a pushover for dogs. I asked about Busybody's cast.

'She's always getting loose and disappearing. She's a real street urchin and isn't happy unless she has her freedom. She came back a fortnight ago with a broken leg. I don't know how it happened, but I think she was probably hit by a car. I was lucky she came home. I rang my vet but it was night and there was no answer so I had to take her to the RSPCA.'

This was my chance to do my sales pitch. I didn't know who her vet was and why he or she wasn't abiding by their professional responsibility but I explained to her that there was a 24-hour

127

seven-day-a-week emergency clinic less than 15 minutes from where we were now standing in case she should ever have the same problem. Today was turning into a real veterinary advice walk.

Smart dogs were everywhere. As we continued towards the open-air theatre an old English sheepdog floated past reading *The Times*. To the right, up Bishop's Avenue, were the **Moat Gardens**. All of this area had once been the Bishop's private game reserve, then later, some time before 1500, the first palace was built. The palace was surrounded by a mile-long moat and curiously, in 1972, Roman coins were found when part of the moat was being excavated. No one knows how they got there.

The force of the gale had been less destructive here and the view, in consequence, was more sylvan. We walked back to the embankment, looking across to Putney. The tide was low and sculls were gliding past in the water. Parked close to the waterline were two motorised waterskis – snowmobiles for liquid surfaces. As we viewed the far side, an apparently unaccompanied Dobermann tore past us, running towards a Rottweiler pup that was burying a body underneath a tree. Both belonged to the same tattooed young man. Tattoos and big short-haired black and tan dogs obviously go together.

Liberty, who had been indulging in her new-found pleasure of mulch-rolling, raced back to us when she saw we were surrounded by a gang of dogs. Four more whippets (not the ones we had just seen near the Pryor's Bank garden), a shiny amber-coated retriever-type dog, three Cavalier King Charles spaniels, three small various mutts and a whippet cross all milled around in the sunshine investigating each other. An Afghan accompanying a pram on a taut lead was walking backwards, bear-like, on his hind legs as his owner refused his imprecations to join in the fun. The amber retriever followed us as we turned to walk back towards Putney Bridge. Lexington liked this dog and after a 'play-bow' they both ran back amongst the fallen branches and leaves to play Catch Me If You Can.

Amber continued with us and Julia became concerned.

'You know my luck with dogs! Listen, dog. Go back and find your person!'

We heard a bark from the football ground end of the park.

'Now, is that someone calling you?' Julia pleaded, but Amber continued with us.

Along the embankment path there are designated exercise stops for walkers and joggers, each with a different piece of apparatus (steps or bars, for example) and written instructions on the exercise you are to perform. All the instructions are hopelessly defaced with kids' 'tags', their desecrating quests for recognition. 'I'M SOMEBODY!' they're trying to say, but in doing so only prove that they are no different from their fellow vandals.

We walked past two borders of plane trees to the central reservation where the tree-surgeons had untied their massive branch and were about to chain-saw it into sections. They told me they were contract workers from Bristol.

'We didn't have any damage in Bristol but as soon as I heard of the havoc in the south-east I drove straight to Nymans to see the damage. I trained as a student there,' said one of them.

Nymans Gardens is a lush and mature conifer and deciduous estate just off the A23 on the way from London to Brighton. 'It was completely devastated,' he continued. 'They lost ninety per cent of their trees. It was impossible to even walk around. Everyone there was so shocked they didn't know where to begin. All the trees I had previously worked on were gone. I drove back home and when I got there a friend from London rang me suggesting that I come down here to help out with the clearing operation. We've been here a month now.'

As he was speaking to us, his partner started up his Stihl chain-saw and stripped the twigs off a branch. He cut three one-foot sections from the branch and, returning to where we were standing, threw one for Lib, one for Lex and one for his own dog.

The sun directly above us caught the wood chips in his curly hair as he spoke with a mixture of resignation with the damage and knowledge of his field. 'All of these trees are going to be lifted into a barge at high tide, over there, and floated down the river. Someone has bought them all but I don't know what they'll be used for.' Park benches, perhaps.

Two other dog-walkers joined us and, after apologising for intruding, they too asked what would happen to the wood and were given the same explanation.

The handsome tree-surgeon grinned as they and their dogs departed. 'Everyone apologises for asking questions but I rather enjoy it. It makes me feel good that so many people are concerned about their trees.'

His junior partner was hovering in the background and clearly

129

needed his assistance, so we rounded up the dogs and moved on.

Amber had, in the interim, fortunately departed. Julia locked her arm into mine and squeezed. 'I'd pile his logs for him *any* time! What a gorgeous attractive man! He went to see his trees at Nymans! Let's go back.'

Dragging her like the Afghan I had previously seen, I moved on, retracing our steps to the ornamental garden. Four men were fishing beneath the bridge on the far side as we paused to view the river. Rather than the more common marshland, there is gravel, Ice Age effluvia, on both banks of the Thames here between Fulham and Putney which made crossing it easier in the olden days and is probably why a settlement developed here in the first place. We crossed windswept **Putney Bridge**, passing three yellowing West Highland terriers on the way, turned past **Putney Pier** and the **Star and Garter** pub, and on to the **Putney Embankment**.

The view from the south side of the river, back over Bishop's Park, was pristine in its clarity, and we could see a wisp of smoke rising from the tree-surgeon's fires. Meanwhile a woman dressed by Burberry's was scolding three Cavalier King Charles spaniels and mallards floated about like vagrants on the water.

At the instant their leads were removed the dogs charged ahead to the slipway down to the river. Lexington launched herself into the water and swam for the sheer joy of swimming, while Liberty barrelled full tilt fetlock-deep along the length of the slipway. They returned to us, shook, and departed. This, at least, was finally cleansing them of their Hurlingham excesses. Lexington swam to each branch in the river as it floated by and dragged it to the shore where Liberty was waiting to take it from her. She smiled a lot.

I called them to me and we continued along the embankment to the next slipway and once more, in the cold wind but under azure skies, they raced back into the water. I worried that they might cut their feet on submerged glass but had some bandage in my pocket in case they did. Lexington continued to clear débris from the water, bringing the smaller treasures to us – cigarette packs, styrofoam bits – while leaving the larger branches for Liberty. Now she was parading proudly around us with something in her mouth, but her prize was invisible. I worried that she might swallow her gift. Commanding her to sit, I opened her mouth, to reveal a water-filled condom.

'Richard Branson's?' asked Julia.

# Walk Eight

## Putney Embankment to Richmond Park

START: The Embankment,
Putney, SW15.

END: Roehampton Gate entrance
to Richmond Park, SW15.

LENGTH: Approximately 7 miles.

TIME: Approximately 3¾ hours.

LEADS: No leads required,
but dogs must be under your
control in Richmond Park.

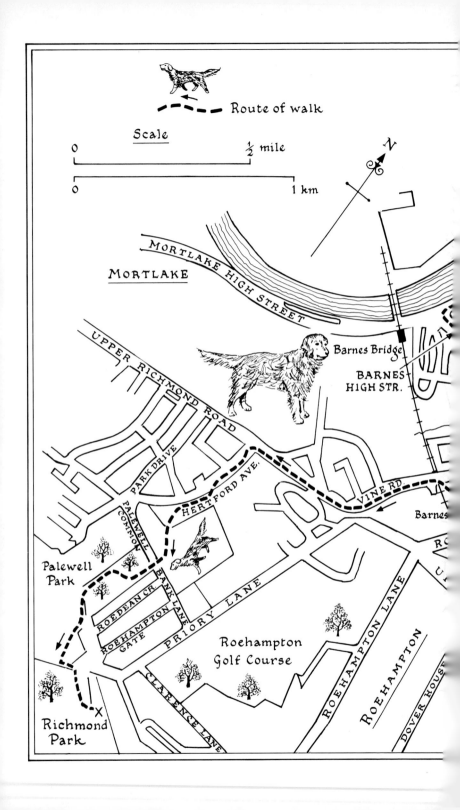

Route of walk

Scale

0 — ½ mile

0 — 1 km

N

MORTLAKE

MORTLAKE HIGH STREET

Barnes Bridge

BARNES HIGH STR.

UPPER RICHMOND ROAD

PARK DRIVE

HERTFORD AVE.

VINE RD.

Barnes

PALEWELL COMMON

Palewell Park

ROEDEAN CR.

ROEHAMPTON GATE

BANK LANE

PRIORY LANE

Roehampton Golf Course

ROEHAMPTON LANE

ROEHAMPTON

DOVER HOUSE

CLARENCE LANE

Richmond Park

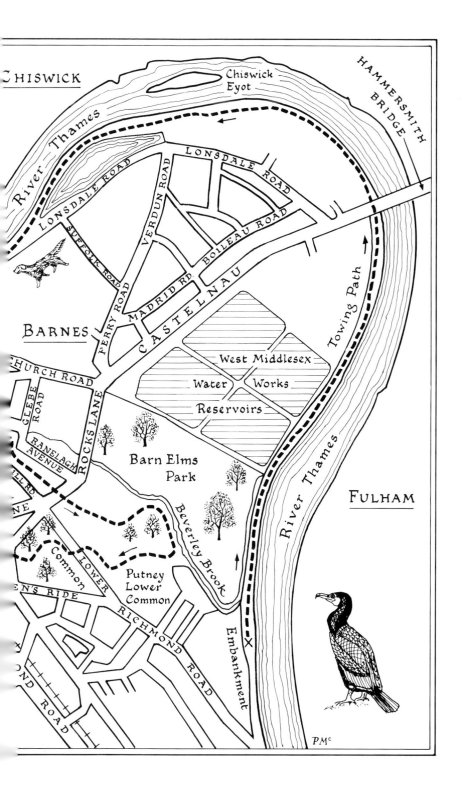

**From Putney Embankment via the Thames Towpath to Barnes, through Barnes Green and Barnes Common to Putney Lower Common, then via Palewell Park to Roehampton Gate and Richmond Park.**

A fog frost lay on the Thames as we set off along the towpath from **Putney Embankment** towards Barnes. The sky was as crisp and blue as a bright winter's day in North America. It invigorated us all with a feeling of well-being – a perfect day for walking alongside the Thames or, in the case of the dogs, swimming from Putney to Barnes. The tide was out, a serendipitous circumstance that allowed Lexington and Liberty to cavort along the gravel river bed by the embankment wall where they danced and fished, oblivious to anything other than their sunshine and water-induced reverie.

Black-headed gulls were feeding on the playing-fields of **Barn Elms Park** to our left. At this time of year, early December, 25,000 to 30,000 of these birds roost here on the adjacent reservoirs every night. It's gull heaven, although not because the reservoirs are good for feeding. Quite the contrary. These migrants from Estonia, Finland and elsewhere find nothing in the relatively fishless water-works reservoirs other than safety and security. They use this spot simply as their nightly roost before flying off to their particular rubbish dumps or open land for their daily meals.

Barn Elms Park itself was once a more wondrous site. A gift from Queen Elizabeth to a faithful retainer, the house gradually fell into decay and in 1884 the fashionable Ranelagh Club, which once occupied the site beside the Hurlingham Club in Fulham, took over the crumbling Barn Elms Mansion and on this site created nineteen croquet lawns, four polo grounds, an eighteen-hole golf course, a five-hole practice course and two lakes. Now it is controlled by the Inner London Education Authority and consists of football pitches as far as the eye can see, with only a few bits of broken statue near the fish pond as a memento of its former elegance.

We had the towpath to ourselves. Where the sun shone the frost was instantly burnt off, leaving snowy crystalline patches only in the shade of the white poplars that lined the walk.

'Liberty! Lexington!' the chief bellowed, and the dogs ran up the sheer precipice from the river to answer their mistress's call. 'Stay up here, now. It's getting too steep for you to climb up and I don't want to send him down there to get you.'

'Him' was me. The dogs looked at me and I acknowledged the command, so they set off on a dash looking for a jogger to knock over. One finally appeared, coming from the Hammersmith Bridge direction, a corpulent man in his early thirties dressed in track shoes, a grey flannel jogging suit, neck towel and sweat. His face was the apoplectic colour of a British Columbia Red Delicious apple and he looked as if he was going to die any second. He probably felt as bad as he looked, for he had long since stopped avoiding puddles and was running in as straight a line as he could, his shoes squelching as he passed us.

'Sit,' commanded Julia as the jogger approached, and we all did.

Jilly Cooper once described the Putney Embankment as the local Devil's Island for neighbourhood dogs. This is where renegade dogs were banished if they were making life difficult for others on Barnes Common and Lower Putney Heath. Her own English setter, a dog that had an apparently insatiable desire for feline flesh, had frequent enforced walks in solitude here. We could now see why. It's a glorious place to walk your dog, but for some reason no one seems to do so.

As we neared the **Harrods Depository** we saw our second human, a lean young man in combat boots and camouflage trousers, jacket and hat, holding camouflage binoculars to his eyes and looking across the river to the outfall pipe from Parr's Ditch, the watery remains of a ditch originally dug to demarcate the boundary of Fulham and Hammersmith parishes.

I walked over to the edge of the towpath and called down to him as he hid in the branches of a willow growing from the embankment wall, to ask him what he was spying on.

'Anything interesting. It's a good spot for birdwatching because of the reeds over there. There are two shovellers. They should be down in Kenya cavorting with the flamingos right now. You'll see just about everything here. Teal, widgeon, sandpipers. Black terns and common terns migrate through here. So do martins and wagtails.'

All I could see were the mallards paddling along our side of the river with my dogs eyeing them covetously. Surface-feeding ducks like mallards, or shovellers for that matter, will eat almost anything. They have comb-like plates in their mouths, one on the upper bill and two on the lower, and by pumping water in and out of their mouths they eat by retaining food in these combs. Shovellers have close-packed combs for catching seeds and plantain, while mallards have wider spaced combs and can eat larger seeds or even small animals.

The phosphorescent sunshine had now burnt off the remains of the river fog and in the middle of the Thames we could see two cormorants cruising upstream. Both dived at once, one surfacing twenty seconds later with a fish in its beak. It was a stunning sight, if for no other reason than this was the first time I have ever had true visual confirmation that there really are fish in the Thames! There in its mouth was a writhing silvery fish, a healthy, vigorous, fresh-looking creature. The cormorant shook it a few times and, turning its bill downwards, took five delicate throws to position the fish head first then swallowed it. Cormorants are deep-diving birds, relatively speaking, which means that they have to have reduced buoyancy in order to dive. They can do this because they have heavier bones than land birds, and feathers that can become more easily waterlogged than, say, the mallards. Which is why they sit so low in the water when swimming, with only their heads showing. Come to think of it, that's why Lexington looks the same. I wonder what would happen if I Scotchguarded Lexington's coat before she went swimming. Would she float like a mallard?

The Harrods Depository is an ominous building. Built in 1894, it looks like an old penitentiary. The extension, equally foreboding in its own modern way, was built in 1969. I explained to the dogs that their wicker beds had once been stored here, but they showed no interest whatsoever and raced off on the path towards **Hammersmith Bridge** with Julia reminding them in no uncertain terms not to even think of going in the water.

It's hard to imagine that the florid, ornate Victorian folly of a bridge here at Hammersmith was built by the same man, Sir Joseph Bazalgette, as the serenely austere Putney Bridge. This bridge was built as the result of an act of Parliament as it was thought that London's existing toll bridges might not be sufficiently safe. As happens to most things, inanimate or living, life has now come full circle for Hammersmith Bridge and it is today the least safe of all London's bridges, with special traffic lights at either end to prevent two buses from using it at the same time! We passed quickly underneath it, one at a time.

**St Paul's School for Boys** lay to our left as we continued along the towpath, but now our path was filled with more obstacles. Trees felled in the October storm had collapsed headlong into the Thames. The dogs crawled under some and jumped over others.

Two more joggers appeared and jogged through the mess. With constant remonstrations to the dogs to stick to the path, we rounded the bend in the river. Stamford Brook, a lost river that has its origins on Wormwood Scrubs and originally fed the lake in Ravenscourt Park across the river, emptied through a conduit on the far side just before the willow-lined Chiswick Island. I called it an island but Julia called it an eyot.

'There are no islands in the Thames from Richmond Bridge through London. There are "aits" and "eyots".'

I asked her what the difference was but she replied with her look reserved for those times when I ask meaningless questions.

'You don't ask why, silly. Those are the names! Look, that's where Faye Dunaway and David Bailey lived.' We were back in estate agent mode as she pointed towards Chiswick Mall.

Two ladies in a scull rowed past and disappeared from view as we continued clambering over fallen trees. There were no people, no dogs, no noise, no nothing. Here we were in the middle of London surrounded by bustling activity and completely by ourselves. The dogs grazed a salad from the grass alongside the pathway, munching through the greenery and the flowering white nettle and vetch. Lexington had been due to come into season a few weeks previously so I didn't discourage her from nibbling the groundsel. An old wives' tale suggests that groundsel, boiled and drunk as an infusion, is marvellous for regulating menstruation. As the dogs grazed, Julia picked winter flowers then jumped Tarzan-like on to each fallen tree, verbally as well as physically reminding me of her excellent balance.

The lime trees that had fallen here were absolutely massive. So were the London planes. One lay twisted and contorted with its back broken over the embankment in such a way that its trunk pierced the water and its massive branches spread like mangrove roots around it. Julia jumped on to it and started walking down into the Thames.

'It feels like I'm on the bow of a great ship,' she called.

'Then get back on to dry land before you get sick,' I replied, knowing that she feels queasy merely standing at a vaporetto stop in Venice.

In the green water of the Thames, the Port of London Authority Harbour Master's launch glided by. The towpath is his responsibility and I shouted down, asking why the walk was still in such a mess.

'Stop that noise at once,' was the only reply. Liberty was barking at something near the waterline and the boss was advising her not to.

Now, for the first time in an hour, we saw a dog, but it was on the Promenade on the far side of the river. In the river, a man in a small dinghy floated past, propelling himself along with a kayak paddle. A pole tied to the back of the dinghy with a microphone on top loomed four feet above him. As we waved at him and he at us, a launch flying the BBC flag drifted past. Julia and I were intrigued by this river activity, but the dogs were far more interested in a small black and white terrier that had come from Barnes to greet them. They offered it bountiful hellos and explained to it in vivid detail how totally dogless their walk had been so far.

As a police launch glided by we departed from the towpath and on to **Lonsdale Road** then **Barnes High Street** where I stopped at a cheese shop and bought a massive piece of Parmesan which we ate in chunks. The dogs yearned for some but I refused as after their repeated swims in the Thames they already smelt like Stilton. We proceeded on to **Barnes Green**, a classically beautiful idyllic rural village green only five miles from the urbanity of the museums in Kensington. Barnes Green had lost its most magnificent willow tree, an ancient of massive girth, large enough for two men to get their arms around.

'That tree-surgeon in Bishop's Park could get *his* arms around it,' Julia commented.

The massive tree now lay in pieces, all the branches removed and the trunk cut into slices.

'I bet he could still save it too!'

Barnes Green was littered with dogs. A latchkey cocker, probably a resident of one of the adjacent homes on The Crescent, acted as head honcho and investigated all the others, striding rather nonchalantly from tail to tail. Lexington sat instantly as he tried to nose under her furry root, while Liberty struck a play position with tail end up and front down, asking the cocker to join in a game. It agreed to do so and they ran into the pond, followed by Lexington, a Labrador and a young boxer. Other dogs stopped to watch the frolics, as did their smiling owners. This was a happy pack of people, amused by the dogs but also thawed by the brilliant sunshine. I am quite convinced that the British are as they are because of the climate in which they live. Reserved and unforthcoming, move them to a warm sunny climate and they become outgoing and verbose. The British are dying to be friendly only it's always dull or raining and by the time the sun comes out again the mood has passed.

On each of the paths criss-crossing Barnes Green were several Barnes women walking several Barnes dogs. Yorkshire terriers, Shih Tzus, Jack Russells, as well as larger dogs – bearded collies, golden retrievers and big mutts – all walked in a dedicated fashion. A marvellous old pub, **The Sun Inn** faces Barnes Green, but the Parmesan had satisfied our hunger, so we proceeded along the green to the bridge over **Beverley Brook** and the beginning of **Barnes Common**. A middle-aged man wearing a Savile Row dark navy suit and black Wellington boots trooped over the bridge with his two cocker spaniels. We said hello but got no response.

Barnes Common is owned but not operated by the Church Commissioners. The Dean of St Paul's is still, technically, the lord of the manor. He leaves its maintenance to the Borough of Richmond, which seems to do a pretty good job of it. Beverley Brook runs through Wimbledon Common and Richmond Park, picking up drainage water along the way, before it flows through Palewell Park and East Sheen to reach here. From here it passes through Putney Lower Common and Barn Elms Park and then empties into the Thames. This section of it was crystal clear, the shallow gravel bed glinting in the sunshine and both dogs flew into it. This is Liberty's idea of water play. She galloped full speed ahead in a straight line, knee-deep along the centre of the channel, then lay down in the brook, whirled around and returned to where she had started. Lexington, in the meantime, was acting more like the shoveller I had not seen and was filtering the surface water looking for things to eat.

We walked along the south bank of the brook, under the leafless branches of the willows and oaks, paralleling **Mill Hill Road**. There is no hill on this road, nor is there a mill, although there were once both. A fascinating aspect of English place names is that they give so much historical evidence about the former uses or features of the land. Beverley Brook is so called because of the beavers that used to live in it, although it is probably a thousand years since the last beaver in this brook was turned into a meal and a hat. The mills, on the other hand, have a more recent history: a post mill stood here until 1780 when it was blown down in a gale and there was a tower mill here also until 1838 when it was torn down.

I returned across the deep and damp grass to the dryer path leading towards Rocks Lane.

'Excuse me, but do you know where Barnes High Street is?' asked a stylishly dressed woman in a violet cashmere shawl.

Julia was at my side in a flash. 'Oh, that's just where we've come from,' she replied as her eyes ran a Grand Prix circuit around the questioner.

A small black and white retriever-type dog poked out its head from behind a tree. Sooni, which means 'the good one' in Korean, was nine months old and, though both looking and behaving like a retriever, weighed less than twenty pounds.

'She's had three previous owners, the first of which was Korean, which is why she is called Sooni, but none of them could keep her. They all still come to visit her and her first owners always bring her gifts,' the owner told us.

Having pointed the lady towards Barnes, I brought the dogs to heel and we walked on past magpies and a jackdaw towards Rocks Lane.

'Are they bitches?' asked an unshaven fellow in his late teens wearing a scruffy black leather jacket and greasy jeans, reeking of tobacco and with tattoos on the backs of his hands. 'I like bitches. They always win the fights. They don't give up the way some dogs do. A dog will walk off from a fight, won't it, but a bitch won't. It will always stand its ground and keep fighting. I like bitches. Are they Labs? I like Labs.'

Julia wasn't concentrating. She was coveting a nearby cast-iron bench.

I replied that the dogs were goldens.

'You're right! Labs are fatter, aren't they? Nice dogs. Do they fight? Cheers.'

By now Julia had full plans in her mind for coming here one evening with her blow torch and paint kit to strip and repaint the bench before dawn. 'It's such a beautiful bench. It's a shame it isn't painted properly. It makes the whole area look uncared for.'

Another magnificent London plane lay dead as we crossed **Rocks Lane**. Others of its species were being cremated in a massive crackling pyre in front of us beside the broodily derelict **Barnes Cemetery**. We walked downwind from the delicious smoke and I took Julia and the dogs into the depths of the tombstone grove. This is a magnificent place straight out of an Edgar Allan Poe story. Even the vividly bright light and crystal clear air today couldn't detract from the spooky feel of the place. Brambles crept over the lichen-encrusted tombstones; dog roses enclosed decaying concrete and marble. The ground was spongy under our feet.

'Oh, we're walking on pine needles. I love it. It's such a magic feeling,' Julia whispered.

I don't know why she whispered. It wasn't a secret. The dogs noticed the pine-needle matting at the same time and both started digging.

'*Not here!*' I bellowed.

Julia kicked through the needles, revealing taut brambles underneath, hidden like Viet-Cong tripwires. Near the centre of this curiously forgotten cemetery (curious because it is, after all, owned by the Dean of St Paul's) grows a giant of an evergreen oak, a pristine fresh emerald island in the middle of the dereliction of angels with their wings and noses amputated. At the very centre of this decay we came across the tombstone of one William Hedgman who died when he was twenty-seven years old. 'His sun is down while it is yet day.'

Leaving the eastern side of the cemetery, we walked through an area that was once allotments and is now dense with the withered remains of frost-killed summer flowers, sycamore saplings and dog roses. This is the muddy and flat **Putney Lower Common**. We turned left and walked along the wooded banks of Beverley Brook. Jilly Cooper in her book *The Common Years* calls this part of the common Flashers Point. So busy is it at the height of the summer season that flashers have to book reservations for the best sites.

The area was dense with stinging nettles, a nuisance, for there was no way we could keep the dogs from running through them and with their coats wet they had lost their natural protection on their bellies. Tonight would be an itchy night for Liberty, who suffers from skin allergies, especially to grass sap, but also to a variety of other types of vegetation.

Having crossed Beverley Brook on the first bridge we returned to our original side at the next crossing and, near the Ranelagh housing estate, turned sharp right back towards Putney Cemetery, clearly visible because of the stately Lombardy poplars that surround it.

The ground was sodden but by now Julia had amassed quite a collection of December wild flowers, including vetch, white dead nettle, dandelion, Queen Anne's lace, yarrow and a sprig of red campion. Two large mutts were sitting beside their Wellington-booted owner who was taking in the sun on a nearby bench and left his side to meet our dogs, who were both pleased to meet some canine companions. All four galloped over the grass, which in plain fact should really be described as marshland. Water and mud flew through the air as they played in the sunshine.

With the dogs on their leads, we crossed **Lower Richmond Road** by Putney Cemetery and returned to a yarrow meadow of gorse, bracken and grass that is technically speaking Barnes Common. Carl von Linné, the Swede who originally classified all living things, the man who named dogs 'Canis familiaris', saw gorse here for the first time in his life and allegedly dropped to his knees and cried. I think it's pretty ugly too.

Both dogs rolled till they were dizzy on the dry grass and Julia wanted to join them. Amidst the birch and pedunculate oak groves an American woman in a grey hooded winter jogging suit and carrying a tennis racket and ball emerged from the bushes, followed shortly by a German short-haired pointer which she immediately tethered.

'Handsome dog,' I offered.

'Have a good one,' she replied.

We marched on through the groves of squat oak and birch. The fields were filled with broom, their dried pods abundant with seeds. The Heathrow flight path was over Barnes Common today and in the lambent sunshine I could almost see the passengers in the low-flying planes.

We were once more at **Rocks Lane** but now near the mulberry red Gothic folly of **Barnes** train station. **Station Road** was lined with BMWs, Mercedes and Escort Cabriolets. After threading our way through these cars we emerged on to a dew-drenched glistening verdant cricket pitch. A nearby bench had been repaired with the boughs of fallen trees and while Julia sat and fantasised that the English team of Mike Brearley was once more representing her country, the dogs investigated the multitudes of worm mounds. Julia picked a few daisies from the grass and we walked on to cross the train tracks, waiting as the barrier came down, an action that Liberty interpreted as the end of the world as she knew it. Lexington, in her own blasé way, failed to notice either the barrier coming down or Liberty freaking out. She was busy observing an Irish setter being walked on the far side of the road.

Once over the two train tracks there is a further grassy area, a football ground, and the dogs were let off their leads so that they could investigate a Cavalier King Charles spaniel and two Jack Russells being exercised by a casually dressed man with more stubble on his face than could be termed designer stubble. The Jack Russells were jumping shoulder high at a proffered stick while the Cavalier rooted like a pig in the peripheral bushes. Lexington went off to investigate the Cavalier, the breed that on her walk across London has emerged as her favourite, while Lib raced over to the Jack Russells, who stopped, sniffed her and both instantly urine-marked twice. These dogs, being so low-slung, were very wet, but that didn't seem to worry their owner.

'You get used to the smell of wet dogs an' all. You forget until you 'ave visitors come into your house and as soon as they arrive they make their apologies and leave straight away.'

Beyond this open ground is a wooded area leading up to Upper Richmond Road. Our dogs had their leads reapplied and as we walked along the edge of the wood near **Vine Road** a sparkling young blonde woman in glasses wearing jeans and a lumber jacket came striding from the thicket. She had snow white incisors the shape of perfect tombstones and the sun shimmered off them. She was accompanied by her chestnut red golden retriever, an obvious American import.

Blinded by the light reflecting from her smile, I found it difficult to concentrate on what she was saying but learned that 'Baca' is Russian for something or other and the dog was ten years old and just out of quarantine. Dashielle, the owner of the teeth with which I was now talking, bought him just outside Boston.

'He's seen me through a lot,' she explained as her eyes flashed with an incandescence in perfect harmony with her teeth. Her flaxen hair strayed in every imaginable direction to reveal hidden in the mayhem several long, neat and very thin plaits.

'I visited him each week at his quarantine kennels near Heathrow Airport. Baca got used to our coming and going. He sort of set his clock to it and was very relaxed but expected our weekly visits. Once, when we couldn't get there, the kennel manager told me that he became restless and anxious when the time of our usual visit passed and we didn't come.'

Beside this flame red retriever my two dogs looked insignificant and anaemic. American golden retrievers are about ten pounds heavier than British ones and far darker, as British ones were at the turn of the century.

Dashielle's comments about Baca's biological clock were sound. Dogs have sophisticated biological clocks that work on a 24-hours basis for daily routine but also on much longer intervals too, weeks in this instance, or even months. Most dogs can cope exceedingly well with quarantine although it is sometimes best that they are not visited at all, which I mentioned to the very feminine lumberjack.

'There was a bulldog at the quarantine kennels – he belonged to a Canadian family – that arrived at about the same time as Baca but his owners decided that it wouldn't be fair to the dog or to themselves to visit him constantly and leave him each time, so they didn't visit him until a week before he was due to leave quarantine. They went out to visit him and he went wild with excitement. He jumped up at all of his family and licked all their faces. He was so overjoyed that he hadn't been forsaken. He jumped into his owner's arms and wagged his tail as fast as he could and licked and licked. Then suddenly he had a massive heart attack and died right there in her arms.'

We often tend to forget that we're not the only species that has emotions. The best dogs to endure the rigours of quarantine are the easy-going ones, the Bacas of the canine world, or even better, pairs of dogs who can give each other constancy in their lives, even though everything else is suddenly and radically different. There is nothing wrong with quarantine as there is absolutely nothing wrong with kennelling your dog when you go on holiday. The significant difference is that on that first experience in a kennels *you* know that your dog will return home but no matter how often you explain that to him he will never know. With frequent kennelling a dog's biological clock sets to the fact that he will eventually return home. Some dogs, especially the more sociable ones, actually like going to kennels, what with the smells, the activity, the noise.

We said our goodbyes and reluctantly moved on. A fox terrier was kicking up earth at the edge of the copse and marking his droppings. As our dogs came into his view he kicked even harder. Julia and I marched our dogs on but they kept turning to look at the terrier who, with each look, dug deeper and started to dig with his forelegs as well as his hinds. This was serious 'bopping' as Julia calls it. As we neared the main road all we could see was a pit with earth flying from it. The terrier had made his point, whatever it was.

The dogs were walked west along busy **Upper Richmond Road** to the first street to the left, **Hertford Avenue**, leading to Palewell Common and Park. The garden of the first house on this very suburban street had gone to seed and the second, I speculated, belonged to a Civil Servant in the Treasury. Every blade of grass was exactly the size of its neighbours. Geometrically placed heather was planted between geometric rose beds and the earth looked like it was turned every eight hours. Nothing was out of place.

A couple of hundred yards along this street, a dog-faeces-littered pathway led through a field of allotment gardens to **Palewell Park**. Carbunculous Brussels sprouts and four-foot-high broccoli rose from the allotments, a ready meal for the neighbouring wood pigeons if a heavy snow this year were to cover their acorns.

'Lovely day,' offered a cocker-spaniel-walker as she was pulled past us.

To our right was a putting green separated from the pathway by a wire fence, and growing amongst the wires were raspberries. Fresh, sweet apple-hard red December raspberries. We picked and ate all that were above Great Dane leg level. Julia leapt the fence to pick daisies on the putting green and I opened the gate to allow her to return to the path. Another cocker spaniel and a Jack Russell tore past, accompanied by smiling owners.

At the bridge leading to the Bank of England playing grounds, both dogs ventured down once more into Beverley Brook and ran to and fro in the ice-clear water. At 1.00 p.m., the park and common were devoid of people and dogs, although on Sundays at this time there are two or three football matches going on, watched by countless big dogs and their owners.

There was still a hard frost on the ground in the shaded areas down the slope to the brook, but the sun was at its strongest and we walked with our coats open and our heads tilted upwards to absorb as much ultraviolet light as possible. In a country as far north as this there are in fact only a few short weeks in June and July when the sun is sufficiently close to allow us to replenish our stock of vitamin $D_3$. That's why the incidence of rickets, especially in children with dark skin, increases as you move north in Britain and also why every single terrapin in the country needs a vitamin and mineral supplement to its diet!

Having crossed **Palewell Common Drive**, we walked as far as we could and eventually came to the brick wall enclosing Richmond Park, where we turned left and walked along its outer perimeter, past graffiti on the wall proclaiming in one-foot-high letters that 'The only true religion is the worship of women'.

Who am I to argue?

I locked arms with the chief and walked into **Richmond Park**. There we saw a golden retriever frolicking in the grass ahead of us, but our hard-working dogs disregarded her. They had spent hours today frolicking in icy water and were now exhausted. I wasn't. The sun was energising and uplifting to me but the dogs were dead and would shortly have even more swimming to do. For every mile we had walked the dogs had probably walked (and swum) three or four, so I reluctantly acceded to their wishes to call it a day.

# *Walk Nine*

## Richmond Park to Wimbledon Common

START: Priory Lane –
Roehampton Gate entrance
to Richmond Park, SW15.

END: Kingston Vale –
Robin Hood gate entrance
to Richmond Park, SW15.

LENGTH: Approximately 5 miles.

TIME: Approximately 2½ hours.

LEADS: Leads not required
but dogs must be 'under your
control' in Richmond Park.

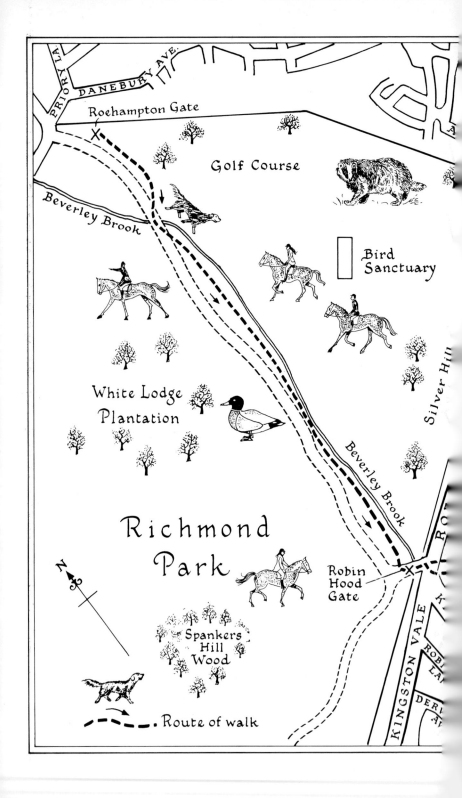

PRIORY LA.

DANEBURY AVE.

Roehampton Gate

Golf Course

Beverley Brook

Bird Sanctuary

White Lodge Plantation

Silver Hill

Beverley Brook

Richmond Park

Robin Hood Gate

N

Spankers Hill Wood

KINGSTON VALE

- - - → Route of walk

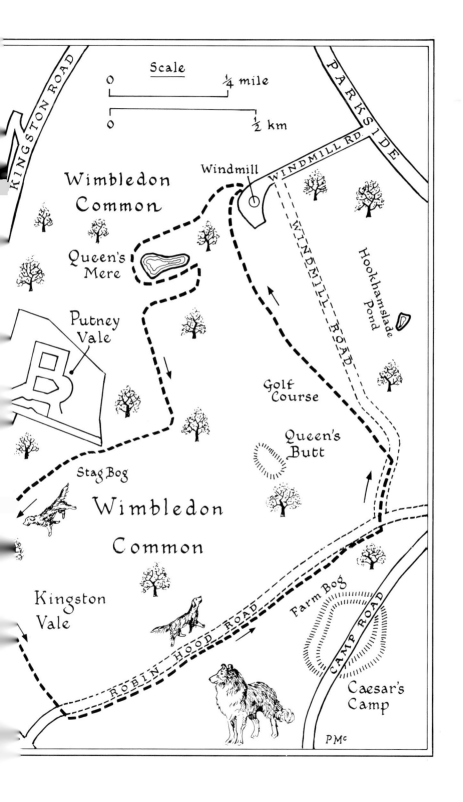

## From Roehampton Gate, Richmond Park, via Robin Hood Gate to and through Kingston Vale and Wimbledon Common, then back to Robin Hood Gate.

The wind was bitterly cold and rain lashed across the park as we set off from **Roehampton Gate** towards Wimbledon Common. This was typical mid-December weather: foul, wet and biting. The rain felt like needles on my face. It probably felt the same to my dogs, but they didn't care. A little wind up their tails was a fine thing. I walked them on their leads until we crossed over the bridge above **Beverley Brook**, then let them off to do as they pleased. They pleased to dive into the water.

Lib and Lex did their ritual spins and loops, exulting in their freedom in the child-like way of all dogs. Julia and I, on the other hand, bundled our scarves around our necks and proceeded along the bank of the brook. A husband and wife both in fluorescent yellow waterproofed jogging suits sprinted past, each with a young Labrador bitch on a lead. The dogs wore matching yellow hair.

Liberty's head appeared above the bank, looked quizzical and disappeared again. Lexington continued dog-paddling upstream, a strenuous feat considering the power of the current. Ahead of her were seven mallards, five drakes and two ducks, all of which departed in a low flight over her head as she approached. She performed a 180-degree turn and power-paddled back in their direction. She didn't know why she was behaving like this, but we did. Lexington is from a successful line of working retrievers. She was bred to retrieve game birds and I have been meaning to train her to her hereditary calling. Her older companion Liberty comes from a line of show retrievers, dogs bred not for their working ability but rather to look pretty. Her flighty temperament is a result of her breeding. She might look handsome, but she's a flake.

The flock of mallards was behaving normally too. It's quite common for there to be more drakes than ducks in a flock. The drakes indulge in communal courtship rituals from now through to spring, preening behind their wings in an obsessive fashion while also raising the wing to show off their black spot, the speculum, to impressionable females. Eventually ducks will bond with specific drakes. This had probably already happened with the mallards that Lexington was following, but the unattached drakes will stick around trying to usurp spoken-for ducks.

At breeding time itself, events become distinctly nastier. A gang of drakes will overcome a drake with a duck and, while part of the group overpowers him, the other half chases, catches and quite literally rapes the duck, who is often left half drowned in the process. So much for sex in the water.

From studies of feather colouring, it has been estimated that one in ten mallards is born as a result of one of these gang bangs. The bonded drake stays with his duck until she lays her eggs, but as soon as that's over and done with he's off. All in all, being a mallard duck is a whole lot tougher than it outwardly seems.

As Lexington neared the flock once more, they flapped and rose above her head, but were again reluctant to leave the relative security of the brook and glided once more upstream. The wind above the banks of the stream was atrocious and they knew where maximum protection lay.

In the distance we saw and heard a black Labrador barking for a stick to be thrown, another retriever desperate to do what human intervention had enhanced in his nature.

Three more mudlarks jogged past us. It was a bleak and blustery day, yet across London these nuts are everywhere. My back hurts just to think of the pounding their spines take. Julia and I continued along the bank of the brook, under the willow, aspen and hawthorn trees. Ahead on the ground I spied a small white egg which I assumed to be a mallard egg, and picked it up. One end of it had been almost surgically incised and the contents sucked out. Somewhere near by was a fox with a pursed mouth!

Julia pointed out pussy willow in flower, far too early even for this earliest of flowering trees. Further ahead, catkins hung from the branches of a hazel tree. December had been unseasonably mild and had confused at least two trees on this river bank into thinking that it must be spring.

Hazels are the standard accompanying trees in oak woods and around us were without a doubt the ugliest oaks in Britain. These are Grimm Brothers oaks, Tolkien oaks, Arthur Rackham oaks. These are the monstrously disfigured odious oaks of morbid fairy tales, the trees that enclose and devour Hansel and Gretel. Some of them have been here since before King Charles I enclosed this land in the 1600s, although they shouldn't be. They should have been gradually replaced over the centuries. Today, left leafless and barren by the horrors of the October gale, their ungainliness and lack of proportion are outstanding. There are others, near Richmond

Gate, that are nearly as unsightly, nothing but thick gnarled trunks with contorted amputated pygmy branches, but none in the park surpasses these oaks from Roehampton Gate to Robin Hood Gate for hideousness.

Riders on horseback trotted by on the roads and trails as we continued in a southerly direction. The dogs were called from their cold shower and pounded through the sodden grass, their feet thundering through the mud. Ahead of us, a golden retriever pup raised her hackles at the sight of the oncoming canine traffic and hid behind her master's legs as my dogs approached. Julia shouted her apologies for our dogs' apparent behaviour but her words were lost in the strong westerly wind. The pup soon recovered her cool and was scampering about with the 'big girls'.

On the flat grassland in front of us, another fluorescent man, orange this time, in green wellies, was throwing frisbees for two border collies, both of whom were expert at catching the plastic discs in mid-air. They were all too busy to be interrupted. The grass was spongy under our feet, but Julia was too cold to comment on it. The wind was blowing the cobwebs away but it would take another half hour or so for her to get out of first gear. The fluorescent yellow man jogged back into view, now with both of the Labradors, who were black with mud and smiling malignantly. There was no sign of his wife anywhere.

At the **Robin Hood Gate** car park, two Irish setters were being let loose and a yellow Labrador was returning to its vehicle. Otherwise the park was vacant but for us and the wind. We put leads on both our dogs and walked them out of the gate to the **Robin Hood roundabout**.

This is the most dangerous spot on our entire sixty-mile walk across London. There is a pedestrian overpass by which you can cross the road but, as an act of fate, a mounted policeman happened by who stopped the traffic for us to cross to the grassy island in the middle and then to the other side. We thanked him and the dogs thanked his horse as we entered the churned-up mud of **Kingston Vale**.

The vale was a bog, the pathway an oozing black soup of ebony earth and horse manure. A park keeper from the nearby playing fields plodded past us and I asked him if it was always so slimy.

'Sodd'n 'orses. Must've bin over three hundred of the sodd'n beasts through 'ere on Sunday. The Tally Ho be'ind the Dog 'n' Fox organised it all for the children's 'ospital. Sodd'n 'orses.'

Rather than stick to the glutinous path, we diverted across the grass to our right and through an opening on to the football playing fields. Liberty disappeared into the hedgerow to reappear twenty yards further up with a water-filled crisp bag in her mouth. Lexington bounced about like a fawn looking for Liberty until she reappeared, whereupon Lex threw her body with delight against the older dog's. Lib has lived without Lex and is happy to go for walks on her own, but Lexington has only known life as a pack dog with Liberty as her 'role model'. She has almost never in her life been taken for a walk in the park without Liberty and as a consequence finds herself lost when Liberty is not there. During the few days after I had spayed Liberty and she couldn't be taken to the park, Lexington was like a child who had lost her mother, anxiously racing home at the first opportunity to be with her boss dog.

'Lexington! Stay out of there!' commanded Julia as the dog eyed **Beverley Brook**. The stream is partly embanked as it passes through Kingston Vale and with the fast flow of run-off water looked too dangerous to enter. Lex reluctantly returned to us as we trudged across the field, passed through another gate from the field and crossed a bridge over the brook to the main pathway once more.

The horses and riders had not come along here, which made it much easier to walk on. We continued along the left bank of the brook, through woodland of oak and birch. Ivy as thick as a tree trunk grew sinuously up a sessile oak, creeping around the branches like a hairy brown boa constrictor. Julia, in the meantime, was pocketing acorns that had been missed by the wood pigeons and squirrels.

'Oh, Bruce. Look! Isn't it awful.'

From the branch of an ancient oak in front of us dangled a heavy hangman's noose. The tree was a classic hanging tree, too, with branches discharging from the trunk at right-angles at just the height that a man could sit on a horse with the noose around his neck. The dogs paid no notice and continued their investigations. Soon they were joined by a German shepherd that sniffed both of them then was off in a flash.

The wind was still howling as we walked past a marker that said 'Paris 186'. Julia asked why there would be a marker here in the woods indicating that Paris was 186 miles away, so we examined it further to see that it actually said 'Parish 1861'. I assume it marks

153

the boundary between Wimbledon (or Merton, as it now is) and Kingston upon Thames.

Liberty had now found a narrow pathway leading along the bank of the brook – a fox run, in reality – and was nosing her way along it. She found what she wanted and proceeded to roll her shoulders on the ground, only to be stopped by thunderous imprecations from her female owner. Lexington trooped down to the spot to see what the fuss was about and, upon scenting the odour, urinated on the same spot.

'Boy, that's strong fox droppings,' I commented to Julia. 'I can even smell it up here.'

Julia couldn't, and she has a pretty good sniffer, so I told her to come over to where I was standing and pointed in the direction of the stench. 'That's not coming from down there, you silly thing. It's coming from you!'

She was right. I smelled my hand and fell over backwards, but where did I pick up the odour? I traced back in my mind what we had done so far and concluded that the odour must have been on the egg I had picked up and that I hadn't smelled it because of the raging wind. Here, in the comparative shelter of the woods, the odour lingered.

I reached down and plucked a handful of grass to rub on my hands but the scent still remained. Foxes are magnificently scented creatures. Apart from having anal glands like dogs and scent glands between the pads of their feet and around their lips like cats, they have a plangent pungent musky urine. This is the smell that we usually associate with foxes, although their faeces also have a distinctively sharp odour. Foxes are, like dogs, canines, but evolved a long time ago away from their *Canis familiaris* brethren. Dogs can still mate successfully with wolves and produce wolf-dogs, but such a feat would be impossible with foxes, as they have a different number of chromosomes to dogs.

Although fox cubs can look almost identical to Pomeranian and papillon pups, they are in fact quite cat-like in their behaviour. Foxes have the agility of cats as well as their stealth; they also induge in scent-marking more than dogs. Dogs scent-mark with their urine and faeces using their anal glands, but foxes scent-mark like cats, rubbing their paws on objects and leaving scent from the sweat glands on their feet. They rub their faces against objects, leaving saliva and scent from the glands around their lips. And, although foxes can sometimes be sociable with other foxes, they, like cats, are lone hunters, as opposed to dogs and wolves, who are pack hunters.

I can't find a satisfying reason why my dogs like to immerse themselves in fox scent. Maybe it's like dressing up in costume. The most popular explanation is that they mask their own scent by acquiring the scent of another animal, but that seems pretty threadbare to me. Dogs like foods that have strong smells. That's why they are such happy scavengers, willing to eat other animals' faeces and decomposing foods. Perhaps there is an in-built delight in any type of strong foul scent, but why?

As I groomed my hands, a couple in their early thirties, both in sensible walking clothes and boots, marched past with two Dalmatians and a spaniel-type dog. The black and white dogs stood out like Technicolor on a black and white background in reverse. I passed pleasantries with the owner.

'When the male gets home he will look as if he hasn't been outside he's still so clean. He has a special radar that tells him where puddles are and he will walk a mile to avoid one. The fat female doesn't like water much either, but she's lazy and would rather walk through a puddle than around it. The spaniel, on the other hand, actively looks for water and will dive into anything that's wet.'

I asked how he came to have the odd mix of dogs.

'We started out with three Dalmatians, but the other male was just too aggressive. The vet tried hormone pills and castration, but that didn't work. We tried behaviour training, but that didn't work either. He was just an unreliable dog that would go for any other dog and sometimes for children. In the end, we had to put him down. It was amazing because the other two became much more pleasant dogs after that. They played with us and with each other more after the other male was gone. It's a hard thing to do, but sometimes it's best for everyone concerned.'

He was right. Some dogs can literally oppress others but we don't see it until the oppression is lifted.

'Listen to that wind!' Julia commented as we moved on. 'It's been getting stronger and stronger.'

The 'wind' was coming from the heavy traffic on the Kingston By-Pass, so we turned left into Wimbledon Common and up a wide dirt track, **Robin Hood Road**, that leads to Cannizaro House at the southern end of the Common.

The track was hard and firm as we started walking up it, but almost instantly turned into a sump of water and black mud. Streams ran down both sides of the path and, while Lexington examined the woods, Liberty wallowed and careened through flowing water catapulting herself through the air when she un-expectedly ran at speed into some hidden brambles. I examined her for skin tears, found none, and we continued on. As I looked at the catkins flowering on the hazel branches here it suddenly became obvious to me why hazel wood is used for divining rods. Hazel flourishes near water. Tamarisk does the same, of course, and actually thrives on water flowing over its roots, but it isn't a dominant tree here as it is around the streams of the countryside I grew up in in central Ontario.

The dogs contented themselves by vigorously tearing apart decomposing sticks and, as Julia hummed 'The Holly and the Ivy', we marched up the trail.

For once, this was an easy word association. We were surrounded by scarlet red berries on holly trees and indigo blue berries on climbing ivy. The former were warding off any evil spirits while the latter were providing a heavy source of winter food for wood pigeons. All that we needed to complete the seasonal picture was mistletoe, the Druids' fertility plant. I walked off into the woods to look for any signs of this parasitic plant but found none in the vicinity and returned to the path where Julia told me to kiss her anyway. She had defrosted.

The wind was still intense but not as biting as before and for a second or two the sun shone, lighting up the woods with a twinkling incandescent colour that just as suddenly disappeared.

The path became firmer as we continued climbing the hill eastwards, revealing the glacial gravels that make this soil so poor for agriculture. Wimbledon Common is a geological accident. Rain soaks through this gravelly soil quickly and in doing so carries most of the nutrients away with it, which is why Wimbledon has remained common land and was never enclosed and is still today one of London's most important lungs. For centuries this area we were now in provided wood and gravel for tenants of the manor. However, as property prices rose in the 1800s, the lord of the manor, Lord Spencer, tried to extinguish local commoners' rights and sell off about three hundred acres for development. Public opinion, led by a local MP, thwarted him and by an Act of Parliament Wimbledon Common and Lower Putney Common passed into the care of a unique group of locally elected and government-appointed conservators. Upkeep is paid for by rates levied on residents who live within three-quarters of a mile of the commons. The closer you live, the more you pay.

Further up the hill, the devastation from the October gale became more intense. The woods had changed from mixed oak, beech and birch to solid birch, and here whole groves were prostrated. Fresh lush ferns grew beneath the damaged canopy.

'Isn't it amazing when you stop and actually look closely,' Julia commented. At her feet within a two square foot area there were four different varieties of mosses, acorns, hazelnuts with more protein gram for gram in them than eggs, rabbit droppings and grass, sand and gravel. In a flash, eight furry legs and two large wet noses were standing and sniffing on those two square feet searching for what we had been looking at.

The gorse at the side of the track was in yellow flower as we crested the rise. Ahead of us, an Irish wolfhound traipsed across the flat open ground. The drainage in this gravelly soil may make the land terrible for agriculture but it's ideal for golf. We were now in the middle of a course.

To the south were the remains of an Iron Age hill fort, known for some curious reason as **Caesar's Camp**. Pottery excavated from this site dates its occupation to between the fifth and third centuries BC, long, long before Caesar was a twinkle in anyone's eye. Ahead of us, beyond the tiny elegant square of houses but hidden by dense foliage, lay **Cannizaro House**, named in an equally arcane manner after Francis Platemone, a penniless and ultimately unfaithful Sicilian nobleman who married the out-rageously wealthy daughter of George Johnstone, Governor of West Florida. Platemone eventually inherited the title Duke of Cannizaro and the house that now bears his name has just become a luxurious hotel.

Liberty found all this information tediously boring, so as I was explaining the facts to Julia and Lexington she took the opportunity to get lost. Julia and Lex both darted back and forth stretching their necks, looking at all horizons. I shouted short harsh 'Liberty's while Julia called her name out like a soprano in a Verdi aria fighting for human rights. 'LIBERTYYYYYYYY.' Lexington ran back and forth not knowing what to do.

'Where do I begin?' she replied with her eyes.

I sent Lex down into **Farm Bog** to look while we checked for any streams that Lib could be wallowing in. The wind was so strong that there was no chance our voices would carry any more than a few feet. Having searched ahead, we backtracked and there, in the distance, we saw her, running like a dart with her nose to the ground back down the path in the direction from which we had come. I was impressed.

'Look, get Libby,' we commanded Lexington and she ran off towards her buddy. Libby caught a flash of her companion in her peripheral vision and turned round to charge back up the hill to us. Julia didn't enjoy that ten minutes.

With both dogs now firmly in view, we turned northwards and, skirting the putting greens, walked past flowering gorse and benches dedicated to lovers of the commons towards the windmill. All golfers here must wear red. It's a local regulation. Dog-walkers, on the other hand, all wear green. There's no regulation. They just do. True to tradition, I was in a green winter coat and off-green cords.

By a stand of pine trees there was a woman in her late fifties with snow white hair and a fine-looking Bichon dog.

'Is yours a tease? Mine is.'

Two miniature schnauzers were being reluctantly dragged along through the damaged pines. They wanted to get back out on the flats where there were equal parts grass and rabbit droppings. In the middle of this flat and golfless area a large black mutt was chasing and retrieving tennis balls being smashed with a tennis racket by his owner into the middle distance. Short blasts of wind-blown rain didn't stop the activity, so I walked the dogs in his direction though advising them to leave the tennis balls alone. He was a big mutt, not one to tangle with.

'I practise my serve and he gets his exercise,' said the owner. 'The only disadvantage is all his slobber on my tennis racket.'

It seemed an apt place to practise your serve, Wimbledon Common. Tennis and Wimbledon are synonymous, but it is only by chance that this is so. Lawn tennis is a relatively new sport. The first match was played in the mid 1800s and the rights to the term 'lawn tennis' were offered to the Marylebone Cricket Club if they formulated rules for the game. This they did. Then they realised that women were permitted to play tennis but were not allowed into the Marylebone Cricket Club. Knowing that the All England Croquet club, south of Cannizaro House on Worple Road, allowed women members, they offered the game to them and that club changed its name to the All England Croquet and Lawn Tennis Club. It was only a short time before tennis came to dominate the club's activities, whereupon they changed their name to the All England Tennis and Croquet Club. The All England Lawn Tennis Championship was first held in 1877 to raise money to repair their lawn-roller!

Our tennis player continued his game, sometimes aiming at the wandering magpies, while we continued our walk towards the now visible windmill. The path here on the height of land was filled with magnificent black puddles and Liberty launched herself into them where she did zippy speedboat turns.

'It's the childlike quality, the innocent childlike joy of dogs that is so appealing,' Julia mused as we watched Lib. 'The same with people, especially men.'

I casually walked over a large sloppy puddle and jumped in, splashing and waving. The dogs loved it and came racing over.

'That's not what I mean,' boomed the chief.

We continued over the drier rabbit savannah to a combe into which the dogs disappeared. The bracken was dense. This, unlike Hampstead Heath, was real heathland, with heather, broom, gorse and dwarf gorse. The best month for bird watching here is April when you can watch pipits parachute down into the bracken and heather. There are at least thirty badgers in Wimbledon Common, too, whose sets are undoubtedly known to the Badger Protection Society. Britain's largest native carnivores need protection because badger-baiting – setting dogs on badgers – unfortunately still goes on.

A path leads down into the combe and up the other side to the flatlands, once a duelling site, to the south of the windmill. As the dogs reached the rise, two Rottweilers on leads tried to attack but were held by their deceptively delicate-looking mistress. I called my dogs to heel, not wanting to second a canine duel today. Besides, these two piggy-eyed hulks would make mincemeat out of my pack.

Duels used to be common on Wimbledon Common. The last one, in September 1840, led to the Earl of Cardigan, later to lead the charge of the Light Brigade at Balaclava, being charged with wounding his opponent. The local magistrates wanted him tried at the Central Criminal Court, but Cardigan exercised his right to be tried by his peers. The trial lasted only a day and he was acquitted.

Much of the flat and relatively arable land on Wimbledon Common was used for vegetable-growing during the Second World War and

159

was tended by Italian prisoners-of-war. The **windmill** itself has its own paramilitary connection in that it was here that Baden-Powell wrote *Scouting for Boys*. This post mill is like the one that used to stand on Mill Hill Road on Barnes Common, and is now the only surviving hollow post flour mill in England. The dogs weren't interested in that but rather in the water bowls put out especially for them, a gentle tradition at the café near the mill.

The parking lot by the mill was occupied by the cars of golfers and dog-walkers. One very old black Labrador with a grey muzzle and opaque sclerotic grey eyes performed both functions, ambling along with a golf ball in his mouth. The bitter cold wind had given both Julia and me an appetite, so I went into the restaurant while Julia sat at a table outside where for some reason twenty-six sparrows chose to congregate, watching her every move and oblivious to the nearby bird dogs.

With soup and baked potatoes in our hands, we turned westwards and walked down into the woods towards **Queen's Mere**. 'Mere' is another of those poetic Old English words that was foreign to me, but Julia explained that it meant 'lake'. There are three 'meres' on Wimbledon Common – King's Mere, Queen's Mere and Rushmere Pond, which, once you know the meaning of mere, seems a bit redundant.

The wind howled through the trees and Julia asked if there were any major roads near by. This time it was the real thing – steady gusting torrents of air through the trees. The dogs dived through the undergrowth and then, seeing the lake at the bottom of the hill, charged down to it. Lexington almost immediately fell in and couldn't get out as the sides were embanked. I got to her and managed to pull her out. She shook on me, then intentionally dived back in again. Around the lake, other owners were pulling their charges from the water too – an Irish setter, a Labrador and Tosca, a very noisy cocker. Their owners were all obviously prepared for water sports, wearing rubber boots and waxed jackets. As we walked to the narrower end of the lake, we saw mallards, pochards and gulls floating in the middle. We reached a natural bank and ordered the dogs into the water so that they could cleanse themselves of some of their mud. As if they needed ordering! Tosca thought this was a good game too and launched herself amongst them, then, as quickly, raced out of the water and back to his (or her) owner.

I chose the westerly path up the wooded hill and all ten legs followed. At the summit we reached two disused **rifle butts** and the edge of the golf course.

'Look!' cried Julia as she pocketed one golf ball then another. Anything on the ground is fair game for her.

The rifle butts are relics of the time when the National Rifle Association held their annual rifle derby here. In front of these mounds once stood targets of artistic running deer that were actually painted by Sir Edwin Landseer. In the nineteenth century, the derby became an important event in the London social season; Queen Victoria fired the first shot of the first derby and Jenny Lind gave a special recital for participants. The only danger from missiles today is from errant golf balls and Julia was busy making sure that the most errant would never be hit in anger again.

Wimbledon Common is reputed to contain every type of native tree in Britain and I wouldn't be surprised if it does. Driving along Parkside gives a false impression that these thousand acres are made up of mostly grassland and marsh. They most certainly aren't and the Common is far more wooded than any other area we'd come through on our walk except for Ken Wood.

As we continued across the open space between the woods, a Borzoi, a dog that looks like it's walking on stilts, lolloped past, followed by a Bichon carrying a log, then the two Rottweilers we had previously seen, still on their leads. They had obviously doubled back to cut my dogs off at the gulch. Lib trotted over towards them and dropped into her 'no aggro – only play' position. They stared at her with their tiny eyes narrowing while their owner pulled their leads and force-marched them onwards.

It must be a real bore to be either the owner of an aggressive dog, always on the alert for danger, or, for that matter, the dog itself, for ever restricted to the end of a lead, never allowed the freedom of movement that comes from having a reliable disposition. Rottweilers are classics. Sure, there are some fine ones, but more often than not they end up in the wrong hands, with people who don't have the ability to train them properly. The owner of these dogs knew she had her hands full, which was why she walked them on leads, and she was good at controlling them on their leads too, but what fun is there in that type of dog walk for either end of the chain?

It was now late afternoon and crows were arriving in small parties in the trees around us. In another hour over a thousand would arrive to roost here at night.

161

A dry pathway led down into the woods so I walked on with the dogs, only to discover after a few minutes that I had now lost Julia. I sent the dogs looking for her, but they returned empty-pawed, so we backtracked, using the same principle that if Liberty had had the common sense to return in the direction from which she had come when she was lost then so would Julia. As we crested the hill we found her sitting behind a tree eating beechnuts.

'I used to collect these when I was a child and take them home and peel them, dry them and eat them. These are already dry.'

Her pockets, already bulging with hazelnuts and golf balls, now overflowed with beechnuts too.

We returned to the path where we met three dirty female Labradors, all with sticks in their mouths and all smiling, together with two elderly and equally smiley ladies, and continued down to where it abutted the **Putney Vale housing estate**. Here we turned left once more on to a muddy riding track and turned right to examine what turned out to be a wholly isolated war memorial to local residents who died in the First World War. A black walnut tree grows near the memorial but the walnuts had worm holes, so Julia left them relatively untouched.

We were back on the playing fields of Kingston Vale, surrounded by flat grassland and mole hills. The dogs were filthy once more but the wind had freshened their owners considerably. Julia found another golf ball, the most errant of the day, and we retraced our steps back to **Robin Hood roundabout** and **Richmond Park**. I took the dogs back to Beverley Brook so that they could wash off most of the mud they had acquired before Julia threw them under the shower at home. It had been a blustery, rainy but still invigorating and enjoyable walk. Perhaps if I live here for another twenty years I'll finally think British and actually look forward to windswept grey days.

In the meantime my roots still overwhelm me and I dream of two days in a row of unending blue winter skies.

# 𝔚alk 𝔗en

## Richmond Park to Ham House

START: Robin Hood Gate,
Kingston Vale,
Richmond Park, SW15.

END: Ham House, Ham Street,
Richmond upon Thames,
Surrey.

LENGTH: Approximately 5 miles.

TIME: Approximately 3 hours.

LEADS: Dogs must be 'under your
control' and must not disturb
the deer in Richmond Park.
Leads required in the Isabella
Plantation and in the grounds
of Ham House.

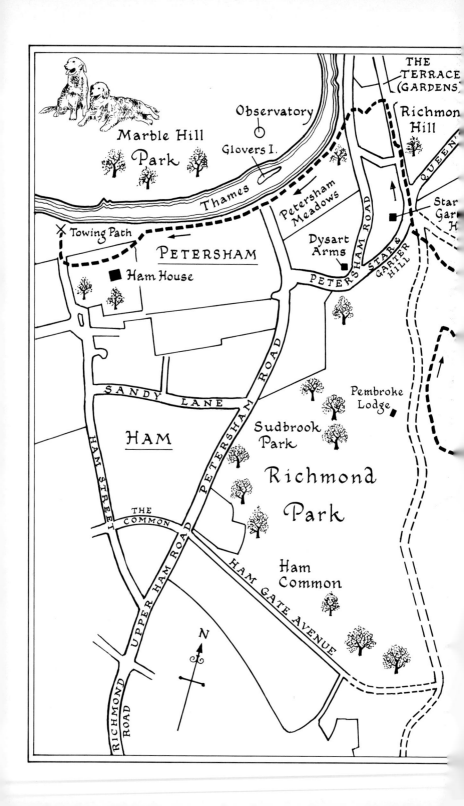

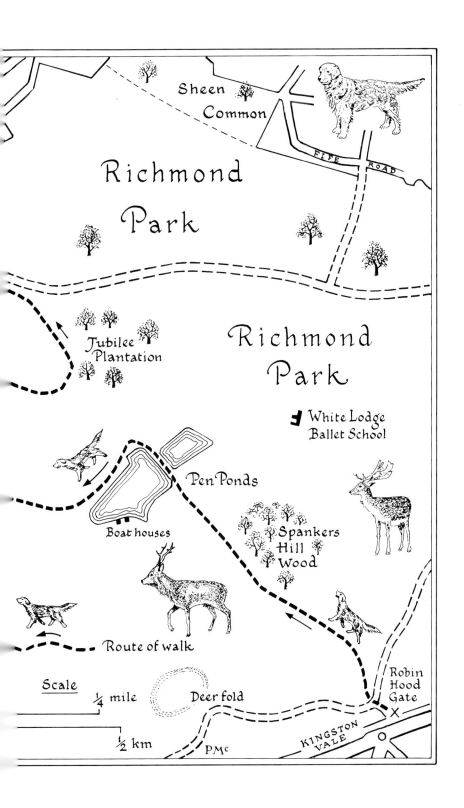

Sheen
Common

FIFE ROAD

Richmond
Park

Richmond
Park

Jubilee
Plantation

White Lodge
Ballet School

Pen Ponds

Boat houses

Spankers
Hill
Wood

Route of walk

Scale

¼ mile

½ km

PMᶜ

Deer fold

KINGSTON VALE

Robin
Hood
Gate

## Richmond Park via Richmond Hill to Ham House.

The avarice and greed of King Charles I in enclosing Richmond Park for his own personal use is why this countryside is available today for dog-walkers, picnickers and deer watchers. Richmond Park is a rare bonus for any city and the cherry on the pie, the ecological jewel in the green crown of London. Almost 2,500 acres of public land with over 200,000 trees on it, so near the heart of a metropolis, is a rare treat. Lexington and Liberty catapulted themselves through **Robin Hood Gate** into the park and on to the cinnamon-coloured bracken in their usual delirium of delight. I felt the same. The great and unforeseen joy of these little walks for me has been getting away from routine, be it the routine of daily veterinary work or the routine of weekend family activity. I charged through the slop, enjoying it as much as they did.

Walking left from Robin Hood Gate would take us along the road and up the hill past the Isabella Plantation. Turning right would take us towards Roehampton Gate. Instead of either of these routes, we marched straight ahead, with **Spankers Hill Wood** to our right, through grass and bracken towards the Pen Ponds.

Lib and Lex ferreted through the rust-coloured vegetation and to their surprise found a perfectly camouflaged golden retriever pup recoiling from their advances. Her owner arrived on the scene and introduced us to Rizla, the six-month-old pup. 'She just rolled up on our doorstep. Geddit? Cigarette paper?'

He was her second owner and she was a fine dog, he told us, but he was unhappy that she feared water. Only this morning, a shivery December Friday, she had fallen through thin ice on a puddle and trembled with fear for minutes afterwards. Lex's and Lib's dominant way of introducing themselves only made Rizla more fearful.

Failing to get a positive response, Lib ran off to act like an idiot in the puddles while Lex stayed and in her more gentle way convinced Rizla to play chase. They scampered like fawns through the grass until Liberty gatecrashed the party. But now Rizla was emboldened and happily joined the twosome as they plunged into the ice-encrusted puddles in the grass. Her owner was delighted.

'You've taught her to love mud. I'm grateful.'

On the grassy slopes of Spankers Hill below the woods themselves there were the feathered remains of wood pigeons everywhere, some with small pieces of fresh flesh still attached. Kestrels pull the feathers out of their kills while foxes chew them out. Judging by the number of feathered patches it had been a busy night in this corner of the park – we counted seven in less than two hundred yards. Earthworms are the main meal of the ever-increasing numbers of foxes in this part of the country. Last night provided richer pickings, however, and I guessed from the sheer quantities of feathered remains that the kills were the work of more than one fox. They'll never reach the numbers that existed where I grew up, though. There, 50,000 wild fox pelts a year was the average kill until rabies reduced the wild numbers and economic forces with perhaps a slight tinge of humanity turned the furriers to farm-raised skins.

Fenced-in Spankers Hill Wood continued to rise to our right as we walked on, a leafless barren canopy over a dense green rhododendron base. Rhododendrons love the acid-rich soil here but this imported evergreen can be an ecological liability. The leaves are too thick for herbivores to eat or sap suckers to suck and they cast such a heavy shadow on the ground that few plants can grow beneath them. The wood is marvellous for burning, however. It's hard to light but keeps a fire going for hours.

'Liberty. Stop that at once,' boomed the commander and I knew exactly what Lib was doing. Rabbit droppings had been popping under my feet since we started walking from Robin Hood Gate. Rabbits don't wander much further than thirty yards from home, so their warren must have been close to where we were, probably on the edge of the woods. The does would be having their first litters now and might go on to produce up to thirty bunnies during the year, although over half of these would die before maturing. The droppings that Liberty is addicted to are actually the rabbits' second droppings. Their first droppings, which are much softer, they eat again as they contain about twenty-five per cent protein. Rabbits' droppings serve three purposes in life: they are a waste product, a scent- and territory-marker and a dog food. I couldn't wait until Liberty sees deer droppings. She won't believe her eyes.

As the Pen Ponds came in sight in the distance so did a lanky Hungarian Viszla.

'Now, there's a fun dog,' I advised Julia. 'Give me this land for my own and I'd raise herds of Nova Scotia duck-tolling retrievers and Hungarian Viszlas. Viszlas are like goldens. They're gentle, relaxed, intelligent and biddable. Good sensible dogs.'

We walked over to the woman who was walking them and she

167

recognised us before we recognised her. It was Sue, who had helped us with our eldest child Emily fifteen or more years ago.

'Bruce, you're just the person! This isn't my dog but I walk her. She's fine with me but destroys her owner's house when left at home. The breeder says that she does this because she gets too much attention and she should be kept in a kennel, but it doesn't sound right to me.'

So much for my description of Viszlas! Neatly avoiding her question, I asked why she was walking the dog if it wasn't hers, and she explained that she was now, among other things, a dog-walker.

'I live in Covent Garden now but I still have to give my dogs their exercise,' she said, 'so I walk the Viszla too and bring them here once a day because it's so easy to park. I take them to Green Park when I can't get here.'

As we talked, a vagrant black dog with a textbook case of flea allergy dermatitis over his rump – corrugated folds of almost bald wispy-haired skin – came over to investigate. 'He's always here. He waits in the car park and investigates everything that moves. I don't know who owns him or if he's even owned but he's a fixture at the Pen Ponds.' The vagabond concluded that there wasn't much interesting on the hill and trotted back down to the car park where another estate car was disgorging its canine load.

There was a misty rain in the air so we moved on, past a lady wearing three dog chains like punk necklaces around her neck and on to the **Pen Ponds** where phalanxes of Barbour-coated, hunter-booted urban 'country folk' were walking their Labradors, goldens, German shepherds and Dobermanns. A lady no older than myself marched past us carrying a young Pekinese dressed in a waxed jacket identical to hers. I asked her why she was carrying it and she explained that the dog hated to get its feet wet but enjoyed visiting the ponds. It looked and sounded faintly ridiculous and reminded me of Martha Scott's comment, 'Don't make the mistake of treating your dogs like humans or they'll treat you like dogs.'

Fishing in the Pen Ponds is by permit only. My dogs ventured in fishing for what water dogs prize – branches and injured or dead birds. There was a thick mulch of decomposing matter on the eastern shore of the upper pond by the path separating the two ponds and as the dogs squashed through it I called out to them, sat them down and told them about the small terrier that in February 1935, while doing exactly what they were doing, got his tail bitten by a pike. As usual they paid no attention.

Pike are fascinating fish. They have grooves on their snouts like the sights on a rifle. In 1940, when these ponds were drained so that the Luftwaffe couldn't use them as navigation markers, over 250 pike were removed from the ponds, as well as 175 carp, 320 bream, 300 eels plus dace, perch and mussels up to six inches long. That seems to be an awful lot of predatory fish compared to prey, but those are the figures. After the war, when the ponds were refilled, pike were not put back in.

We nodded and said hello to other dog-walkers, all of whom mumbled back their hellos but continued on. All were silent, like figures in a Lowry painting. The dogs charged down and into the lower pond where swans raced over to see if they were edible. Julia implored the dogs to return to her.

'Look at that swan's neck. He could break your leg with it.'

In my final summer at veterinary school, one of my jobs was to give intravenous drips to seriously injured swans brought in from the local waterfowl refuge. Getting the needle into the wing vein and strapping it in was the easy part. These were sick birds. But after a few hours floating in a bathtub with rich nutrients pumped into their veins it was a different story and I learned to have a deep respect for their powers.

As we stood on the high path by the lower pond a gaggle of Canada geese flew in from the direction of the White Lodge, beyond the rise to the east. The Lodge is now the residence of the Royal Ballet but at one time it was King George II's hunting box. Queen Victoria moved there to recover her composure after her mother died. It was also the birthplace of King Edward VIII. The old Hanoverian King George must have been a lazy hunter. In the area from which the gaggle had arrived, George kept over 3,000 almost tame turkeys and, when the mood took him, he would let loose his dogs, which chased the birds up the trees where they were then shot by George.

There are supposed to be barn owls, little owls and tawny owls around the Pen Ponds, but that would have to await a night-time visit. My original plan had been to go from here to the left of the upper pond and on to and through the Isabella Plantation, but it was temporarily closed because of storm damage. This didn't bother the dogs, as they must be on leads in the plantation, so, missing the magnolias and camellias, azaleas and rhododendrons, we headed due west along the right-hand side of the upper pond, over spongy grassy turf until we reached **Whiteash Lodge**.

Now was decision time: whether to continue right to Ham House via Richmond Gate and Richmond Hill or turn left towards Ham Gate with its quaint cluster of cottages leading to the long flat rural woodland walk through Ham Common to the village green, from which a narrow riding path would lead us to the old Jacobean mansion. If the weather had been less inclement I would have chosen both, walking to Richmond Hill first then down through Petersham Park to Ham Gate. It was too threatening for that extra hour, so I commanded my pack to turn right and walk paralleling the road, past **Pembroke Lodge** – now a residence and restaurant but originally the Royal Mole Catcher's home – and along the edge of **Sidmouth Wood**. There had been an agglomeration of mole hills on Kingston Vale but we hadn't seen any in the park itself – perhaps a sign that there isn't the need for a royal or even common mole catcher any longer.

My dogs, in the interim, were investigating the perimeter deer-proof fencing around the wood and finally discovered the deer-proof gate where they were both sitting, waiting for one of us to open it. The gate was almost dog-proof, too, allowing only the most supple and bendy long dog to slip around the narrow U-bend. Lexington did this with alacrity but Liberty was less inclined, so Julia had to shove her through the gate.

The wood, named after the deputy park ranger who in 1823 enclosed and planted it, had been ravaged by the gale. Out on the open grasslands of the park there had been grave destruction to the branches of the stockaded trees and some trees were down, especially near the walls, but here in the dense woods we were surrounded by debris. This was a delight for the dogs. They swept down **The Driftway**, diving under and sailing over fallen sweet chestnuts and beeches, and running through the surrounding rhododendron bushes, disappearing for minutes at a time. As they did so, the wood pigeons, as one, took flight. Now, something that has always amazed me is how animals pass on a danger signal instantly to each other so that all run or take flight at the same time. When mallards roost, for example, each one will, at intervals, open its eyes. This means that at any given time one bird or another will have its eyes open and will spot danger. Roosting wood pigeons have a common alarm signal, too. Normally, when a wood pigeon is about to take flight, it signals its intention to do so by crouching first before take-off. If it doesn't crouch, if it doesn't display that 'intention' movement and takes off without doing so, the other birds are alarmed and the flock disperses. My dogs don't look exactly like foxes but after the previous night I guess these birds weren't taking any chances with anything smelly, furry and on four legs.

The type of grave destruction that had befallen Sidmouth Wood must leave the park superintendent in a quandary. When isolated trees in the grounds fall down, it is obvious that they should be removed and new trees planted, but the natural destruction of a dense wood is another story. In the central woods of Ontario, for example, the white pine was, until the turn of the century the most dominant tree, but once it was logged to depletion it never returned. The reason was because after the pines were removed birch and cedar – opportunist trees – moved in and took their place. More importantly, forest fires were controlled through human intervention. White pines actually rely upon forest fires to regain supremacy over the land. The heat of a forest fire opens the cones of the pine and allows its seeds to spread while the fire itself destroys the opportunist trees and provides the white pine seedlings with the light they require to grow.

The problem that arborists throughout the south of England face is, do they allow a natural regeneration or do they intervene?

When there is a wood fall, there are other natural advantages, for dead wood is an important base for the pyramid of life in the woods. Dead wood, especially large timber such as there was here, will provide shelters for bats and other mammals. It will initially be decayed by fungal growth which in turn will make it digestible for many insects. This in its own turn will attract insect-eating birds like woodpeckers. The gap in the forest canopy will allow light in, forming a glade in the woodland. When this happens, the herb layer at ground level will suddenly thrive and flowers that are adapted to shade living will flourish. Primroses and violets, for example, should seed better, if for no other reason than that they are more likely to be visited by pollinating insects. Butterflies may also increase, as they favour warm sheltered glades rather than darker woods.

The natural cycle will continue with saplings taking root while the ground cover becomes thicker, providing cover for ground nesting birds. Eventually, the canopy trees will emerge triumphant once more. It may take a hundred years, but the natural forest will return.

As we continued on the trail through the wood, heading back

towards the Pen Ponds, we came to a massive fallen oak and pulled ourselves over it. This tree had obviously been here from before the plantings in the early 1800s. Standing high on its prostrated trunk I surveyed the woods ahead. Acorns and leaves were inches deep on the ground around me but Julia, resisting temptation, was contemplating whether to go over or under the massive hulk. An oak of this size probably produces several thousand acorns a year. This one had done so for hundreds of years. That's a lot of acorns with nothing to show for it when you consider that only one of those hundreds of thousands has to seed and survive for the tree to fulfil its biological requirement to repeat itself.

As we continued along the pathways the number of obstacles increased. Julia commented that there must have been even worse destruction in the Isabella Plantation for it to be closed to the public. Then, as we neared the eastern exist from the wood, she stopped in her track.

'Is it or isn't it?'

The question concerned some mushrooms the colour of an egg yolk with many folds to their caps. There were three of them, growing in the moss on the sandy soil near an old oak and the question was whether they were chanterelles. Julia picked the smallest one and stuffed it under my nose.

'Smell it,' she asked, occluding my nostrils.

It had a pleasant odour, not unlike apricot, and I diagnosed that her supposition was correct and asked if it would end up in an omelette that evening.

'What if it's poisonous?' she continued. 'What a way to end the walk.' So she threw it away.

The wood exit gate was similar to the entrance on the other side, but now Liberty was experienced so she glided through this one. Facing us were the reflective grey Pen Ponds and to their left in the distance the dreary view of the Le Corbusier-influenced Alton Estate at Roehampton. It is remorseless, dull, Soviet and utterly unavoidable from this side of the park and crushes the feeling of being lost in the countryside.

Turning left we walked around the periphery of the wood towards **Queen's Ride**, a trail leading from the White Lodge to Richmond Gate. However, I lost Julia to a sweet chestnut tree.

'You told me there are 2,000 squirrels in this park but they haven't found *this* tree,' she cried with glee as she pocketed small unopened unmarked sweet chestnuts.

As I had gloves on, I was given the responsibility of removing the hard nuts from their prickly dried brown-green containers.

'They must have all fallen at once in the storm. You *never* see so many in one place and *never* at this time of year. *Never ever.*'

There was a subtle degree of the positive in her voice.

As we stood under the overhanging tree a robin arrived and sang its heart out. It sounded pretty but was probably a warning to other robins that if they came anywhere near *his* tree he'd have their guts for supper. Each robin song has four parts or phrases to it and the bird is capable of producing hundreds of phrases. By recording these songs and then chopping them up into phrases, remixing them and playing them back, ornithologists have learned a little about the way robins sing. Consecutive songs, for example, must be different and the phrases must have alternate high and low pitches. It's possible to electronically put together a series of sounds that will provoke an aggressive response from a territory-owning robin. This particular robin was not, however, telling us to lay off his nuts. As an insect-eater he was probably astute enough to realise that our shovelling through the fallen chestnuts would leave a trail of exposed earth littered with available insects.

On the rise between Sidmouth Wood on our left and the **Jubilee Plantation** on our right, my dogs, for the first time in their lives, saw deer droppings. I was deflated. They did nothing: a peremptory sniff and they were off. In the dip on the other side of the road was a herd of dapple fallow deer drifting like a grey cloud over the meadow. To their right a magnificent red stag lay in the grass chewing his cud, surrounded by his harem. About thirty of these noble animals are killed by cars each year in the park, sometimes as they run from dogs, so I was content initially to view them from afar rather than move any closer. The fallow deer still had their summer spots but they were fading gradually into grey winter coats. Only the males have antlers, which are distinctively flattened at their tips. Fallow deer have rather long, distinctively striped tails and black margins around their white rumps. They were grazing under the stockaded oak trees, probably eating heather and acorns.

Dapple fallow deer look small and delicate, Bambi-like, compared to the noble red deer. In order to prevent them from chasing the deer, the dogs of the district used to be 'expedited' or 'lawed', which involved cutting off the front three claws of their forefeet close to the ball of the foot. My dogs obediently sat shivering beside me and didn't budge an inch as I explained.

It might appear that the deer are here for show, but they are in fact farmed for the royal and diplomatic tables. The holders of certain offices are entitled, by royal venison warrant, to a specified amount of venison each year. The Prime Minister and the Archbishop of Canterbury are each entitled to a quarter, whereas the Lord Mayor of London is entitled to four quarters which, according to my calculator, is a whole deer. His larger entitlement dates from the Civil War. After King Charles I, the usurper of these lands, was dethroned and executed, the park passed into the ownership of the citizens of the City of London. After Cromwell and the Restoration, however, the citizens of London thought it expedient to hand it back to King Charles II, who returned the favour by supplying the Lord Mayor with a little food, in perpetuity, for his table.

The last great outbreak of rabies in London occurred near where we now were, just over one hundred years ago. In September 1886, a fawn suckling a doe was seen staggering about near East Sheen Gate. That's the site of Sheen Cottage, originally called the Dog Kennel, just the other side of the wall we came to when we were walking across Palewell Common and approaching Richmond Park.

The keeper killed her and noticed that the doe had rubbed the hair off her head. Over the coming months, other does died too, self-mutilated, hairless and torn by other deer. Post mortems revealed that their stomachs were filled with sticks and other indigestible objects. In the spring when the bucks lost their antlers, they too started dying. Until then they were able to fend off rabid does with their antlers but now, without their protection, they too became infected and passed the virus on through saliva-tainted skin wounds to others.

By April of 1887 over 160 deer had died and in the next five months over a hundred more perished. Today, of course, it would take nowhere near as long for a diagnosis of the cause of the epidemic to be known. These deer had the classic signs of both dumb and vicious rabies. Any dairy farmer in Ontario would know the signs – salivation and lassitude or aberrant rage – because rabies is a constant threat to his cattle through rabid fox bites, but one hundred years ago, here in Richmond Park, it took a year before the cause was determined.

Rabies probably affected the herd through an initial bite from a rabid dog. The fact that such a prolonged and massive outbreak was contained and didn't spread permanently to the wildlife reservoir for the virus was a chance of fate rather than the result of detailed planning, but this event was undoubtedly in its own way responsible for the development of the slaughter policy which is in effect today in the event of another rabies outbreak.

I wanted to have a better look at the red deer, so Julia kept the dogs by her side while I crossed the road. It's dangerous to approach deer during the rutting season in October and November or during calving in the spring. It can be dangerous, in fact, at any time so I approached slowly and calmly. The massive buck had two tines projecting forward from near the base of his antlers, the sign of maturity that younger males do not have, and he kept chewing his cud and watching me out of the corner of his eye. The does arose and walked away as I approached, so I moved no further. I looked at those massive antlers wondering what would happen to them in the spring when he shed them. Julia has big pockets in her jacket but this would stump even her.

The stag arose and almost mindlessly browsed and grazed as I returned to my own herd, who were all looking alert and expectant. I've never administered to wild deer although one of the first cases I treated when I worked at Regent's Park Zoo eighteen years ago was a foot injury in a Père David deer. They're noble-looking animals, appropriately regal for this royal park.

**Kidney Wood** near **Richmond Gate** was plastered with 'dangerous tree' signs, as if they were about to charge triffid-like across the road and out of the gate to eat Richmond. We put the dogs' leads on for the first time that day and walked through the gate and past the **Star & Garter Home**, the site of a hotel where Charles Dickens came yearly from his home in Tavistock Square, Bloomsbury. In fact, he came here in 1850 to hold a dinner party in celebration of the publication of his book David Copperfield.

On the right of the road there is an old ironwork pavilion surrounded by a water fountain with the water coming from spigots in the shape of dogs' mouths. It seems rather inappropriate considering the history of rabies in the area and was placed here by the Richmond chapter of the Royal Society for the Prevention of Cruelty to Animals. It's now a circular flower trough.

From **Richmond Hill**, above the Terrace Field and Gardens, we looked over a misty panoramic view of Kew Gardens and Syon Park to the north, Hampton Court Park and Bushey Park to the south and Ham House and gardens to the west. Behind us lay a splendid row of Georgian buildings, in all surrounding us with

175

what on a sunny day must be one of the more glorious sights in London, if not in all of Britain.

Looking down from the heights of the hill we saw Holstein cattle grazing on Petersham Meadows and German shepherd dogs leading their masters along the pathways through Terrace Field.

Beside us was **Wick House**, with a conservatory I wouldn't mind as a home, built originally for Sir Joshua Reynolds of the Royal Academy and now a nurses' residence.

We walked across **Terrace Field**. Liberty slipped into Terrace Gardens and drove down to its bottom, only to be recalled to join us on the less elaborate side of the fence. At the bottom of the field a debonair black man, perhaps in his mid forties and wearing a blue cashmere coat, held the gate open for us.

'I do hope you are enjoying your walk today,' he offered in a velvety BBC voice as we passed through. We assured him that we were.

'Out-of-work actor. The place is riddled with them. Richmond is a favourite for actors. John Mills lives somewhere up there on Richmond Hill,' Julia explained as we crossed **Petersham Road**.

At the towpath by **Petersham Meadows** we turned upstream, past ardent and determined fishermen none of whom had caught anything in the turbulent waters. Many people were walking their dogs here but they were doing so in a busy fashion. There is no time to stop and dawdle when walking a towpath and the mutts, collies and two pristine clean snow white Westies and their owners all moved along briskly and silently.

As two elderly ladies walked past faster than the others Julia nudged me to turn around and look at their knapsacks.

'They're not knapsacks. They're rucksacks,' explained my English wife. 'Knapsacks are canvas and are used by soldiers. Rucksacks are cotton and carried by sensible English ladies wearing sensible walking shoes.'

As Julia threatened the dogs with sudden death if they entered the river, I walked along the top of the fence separating the towpath from the lower water meadow in which some Holsteins were grazing. Later on that day these cows would be milked, as they are every day, in their milking parlour on River Lane. The dogs raced over to me and bounded over the wall, landing in deep piles of cow manure. I ordered them back over the wall and as we approached **River Lane**, let them dive into the Thames to cleanse themselves. The discoverer of British Columbia, Captain George

Vancouver, after whom the most magnificently situated city in North America is named, retired to River Lane and is buried in the churchyard of nearby St Peter's Church in Petersham.

It was obvious from the detritus on the towpath that there can still be high floods on this part of the river. The easiest way to determine the maximum flood level is to look for the highest level of styrofoam on the banks.

The walk was soon to be over. We approached the first entrance to the riverside grounds of **Ham House**.

'I know this place!' asserted Julia. 'This is where Anne had her fiftieth birthday party. Don't you remember?'

I didn't remember going as I'd been away at the time but I was astonished that you could actually book this great Jacobean pile for private functions. In front of us two horses and a golden retriever-type dog were being exercised in a horse ring. The dog was happily learning to jump an obstacle course. My dogs looked at each other and winked. 'Kids' stuff,' they thought as they recollected the barriers they had overcome in our walk across London, in which the dogs had covered at least two hundred miles to Julia's and my sixty.

On the lawn in front of us were six fallen trees prostrating themselves before the Thames. Others had by now been cut and removed and were being burned in a large fire close to the river.

'We'll never again in our lives see wood like that simply being burned for no apparent use,' Julia whispered to me as we walked past the fire of pristine logs. Out of the dogs' way hopped two magpies – these birds had already paired for the winter, ready for spring mating. A retired-looking man approached from the opposite direction and, as my dogs went to investigate his, he picked up his wool-coated miniature poodle lest it be contaminated by my filthy beasts. A mother and child walked past with their small black mutt, a happy dog that was delighted to be investigated by Liberty and Lexington. 'I always like a little mongrel myself,' George Bernard Shaw once commented and he was right. On our walk through the heights of designer London, I'd seen more mutts than any specific breed.

'Where's the champagne?' Julia asked. 'Oh, you're so unimaginative,' came her reply as I shrugged my shoulders. 'Now listen. I know the walk across London is over but we're not stopping here. We're going to continue doing this. It's been glorious fun.'

This from the lady who was born with four wheels rather than legs was a startling admission.

'How about the High Sierras then?' I countered. 'Just a week. You, me and the dogs. The only problem is once we take the dogs over there we won't be able to bring them back so we'll have to stay. Whad'y'a think?'

The boss was silent. She was born here. She actually likes cloud and rain. We walked into the riverside car park. The dogs eyed the swollen river. I thought of bright skies and warm sunshine. The reverie lasted only seconds.

'Don't even think what you're thinking! Lexington, Liberty, Bruce! Into the car!'

# Postscript

As a curiosity, I kept track of the dogs I saw while walking across London and classifed them according to breed. Cross-breds were by far the most popular 'breed'. There were 175 of them but they were still in a substantial minority compared to the total 311 pure-breds I observed on the route.

The top ten pure-breds were:

| | | | | |
|---|---|---|---|---|
| 1. Labrador | 35 | 6. West Highland terrier | 16 |
| 2. German shepherd | 29 | 7. Jack Russell terrier | 15 |
| 3. Cavalier King Charles spaniel | 24 | 8. Yorkshire terrier Dobermann | 10 |
| 4. Golden retriever | 22 | 10. Border collie | 8 |
| 5. Cocker spaniel | 21 | | |

According to the Kennel Club, the most popular breeds of dogs in the United Kingdom in 1987 were:

| | |
|---|---|
| 1. German shepherd | 6. Dobermann |
| 2. Labrador | 7. Rottweiler |
| 3. Golden retriever | 8. Cocker spaniel |
| 4. Yorkshire terrier | 9. English springer spaniel |
| 5. Cavalier King Charles spaniel | 10. Staffordshire bull terrier |

It was interesting to see that my dog 'sample' quite accurately mirrored the nationwide statistics. I saw lots of Jack Russells, which are popular dogs in my veterinary practice. The Kennel Club, however, doesn't recognise this breed which is why it doesn't appear on their list.

The Rottweiler is rapidly becoming one of the most popular breeds in the UK, currently standing at number seven in the league table, but I didn't see many and those I did see were firmly tethered to their walkers. This probably says something about the breed's temperament. Their sudden popularity has brought with it a severe behaviour problem – unprovoked aggression. There might

179

be lots of Rottweilers around but they're not suitable for free exercising in dog-crowded London.

I learned from the walk that agglomerations of canines occur in the parks first thing, between eight and nine on weekday mornings, and then again after one in the afternoon. However, Sunday is the best day to observe dogs and dog-walkers everywhere in London, although even then early morning is as good as late afternoon.

Dog-walking is part obligation, part excuse. Dogs need to be exercised, but in walking them you too have a chance to slow down, to let the beat of your heart set the pace of your activity. And if you do so in the right spirit, you can become as keen an observer of the natural world around you as the most experienced canine.

# INDEX

# INDEX

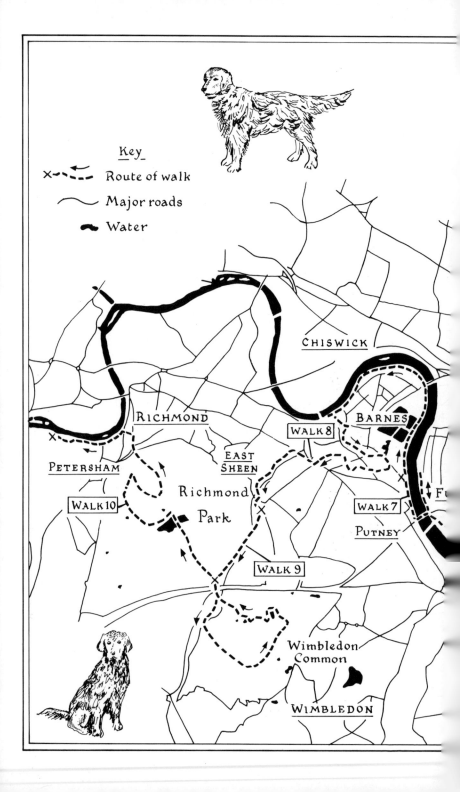

Key

×⋯⋯ Route of walk

⌒⌒ Major roads

⌒ Water

CHISWICK

RICHMOND

BARNES

WALK 8

PETERSHAM

EAST
SHEEN

Richmond
Park

WALK 7

WALK 10

PUTNEY

Fu

WALK 9

Wimbledon
Common

WIMBLEDON